# SHADES OF REALITY

# SHADES OF REALITY

## How the New Fuzzy Philosophy Will Change *Your* World View

### Bob Bishop
### *(Mr. Logic)*

Glenbridge Publishing Ltd.

Other Books by Bob Bishop

*Applevisions: A Unique Introduction
to Assembly Language Programming*

*Programmers Assembly-Language Construction Kit (P.A.C.K.)
Vols. I & II*

Copyright © 1998 by Bob Bishop

All rights reserved. Except for brief quotations in critical articles or reviews, this book or parts thereof must not be reproduced in any form without permission in writing from the publisher. For further information contact Glenbridge Publishing Ltd. 6010 W. Jewell Ave., Lakewood, Colorado 80232

Library of Congress Catalog Card Number: 97-74302

International Standard Book Number: 0-944435-44-0

"To You
Just as you are —
*Perfect*
In your imperfections"

# Contents

*Preface* . . . . . . . . . . . . . . . . . . . . . . . . . . . . . . . . . . . . . . . . . . . xi

Introduction to Reality . . . . . . . . . . . . . . . . . . . . . . . . . . . . . . 1

Chapter Zero:     Consistency and Correctness . . . . . . . . . . . . 14

### Part One
#### The Foundations of the Fuzzy Paradigm

Chapter One:      The Smoothness Principle . . . . . . . . . . . . . . 32

Chapter Two:      Categorization . . . . . . . . . . . . . . . . . . . . . . . 42

Chapter Three:    Fuzzy Logic . . . . . . . . . . . . . . . . . . . . . . . . . 55

Chapter Four:     Truth and Knowledge . . . . . . . . . . . . . . . . . . 68

Chapter Five:     Fallacy and Paradox . . . . . . . . . . . . . . . . . . 81

Chapter Six:      Fuzzy Words and Fuzzy Existence . . . . . . . . 93

### Part Two
#### The Social Implications of the Fuzzy Paradigm

The Kingdom of Aristotelia . . . . . . . . . . . . . . . . . . . . . . . . . . . 108

Chapter Seven:    Fuzzy Logic in the Real World . . . . . . . . . . 114

Chapter Eight:     The Laws of the Land . . . . . . . . . . . . . . . . . 130

Chapter Nine:     Realistic Law . . . . . . . . . . . . . . . . . . . . . . . . 143

Chapter Ten:      Legimetry . . . . . . . . . . . . . . . . . . . . . . . . . . . 159

Chapter Eleven:   Abortion . . . . . . . . . . . . . . . . . . . . . . . . . . . 174

Chapter Twelve:   Rights and Equality . . . . . . . . . . . . . . . . . . . 191

Chapter Thirteen: The End . . . . . . . . . . . . . . . . . . . . . . . . . . . . 206

*Appendix* . . . . . . . . . . . . . . . . . . . . . . . . . . . . . . . . . . . . . . . . 216

# ACKNOWLEDGMENTS

### Geri Bishop Davison

My personal manager, agent, and
best friend, whose efforts made
the publishing of this book
a reality.

### Scott Davison

**Daren Davison**

# Preface

As "Mr. Logic," the talk show host of KSCO's *Thinking Machine,* I have had the opportunity to discuss many of the new topics in science and technology. But the one topic that my listeners have the greatest trouble comprehending is not the Big Bang theory, nor is it the idea of multidimensional universes. Surprisingly enough, the concept that gives them the most trouble is the simple notion of *shades of gray*! Perhaps because the idea *is* so simple, it's difficult to extrapolate it past the obvious.

While the new science of fuzzy logic is gaining acceptance in the field of engineering, the American public at large is, for the most part, completely ignorant about it. And even those who *have* heard the term "fuzzy logic" think that it merely refers to nothing more than some new branch of "electronics."

I discovered the concept of fuzzy logic, not by reading about it, but by thinking about it on my own. Several years ago I had not yet heard the term "fuzzy logic." Instead, I had been discussing on my radio show a concept that I had come up with a long time ago — a way of thinking that I urged my listeners to avoid. I referred to this undesirable way of thinking as "all-or-nothing-ism," a mind-set that I would later discover represented a form of Aristotelianism.

xii     *Shades of Reality*

Because my paradigm of a gray reality was not fostered by the seeds of "mainstream" fuzzy logic and its engineering-only applications, I have been able to extrapolate the concept of "fuzzy" further into the philosophies of everyday life than most other authors in the field have done. Hopefully, this fresh approach will inspire an even better understanding of our perceptions of reality.

I have decided (with great trepidation) to divide this book into two "parts" even though such an Aristotelian partitioning is contrary to the very *theme* of the book. But even the subpartitioning of a book into "chapters" is a convention, which most authors utilize for the sake of convenience to their readers.

The first part deals with the more conventional aspects of fuzzy logic (with a few new twists of my own), while the second part discusses the more revolutionary ideas that result when the fuzzy paradigm is applied to societal issues. Many of these ideas are going to strike some readers as rather strange or foreign, and the concepts will definitely not be in accord with how most Americans have been brought up to think.

Hundreds of years ago mankind thought that the earth was the center of the universe. They looked up at the sky and saw that the entire universe revolved around the earth once every twenty-four hours! And then Galileo pointed a telescope at the planet Jupiter one evening and saw four tiny pinpoints of light revolving very slowly around something *other* than the earth.

I've often wondered, if I had been alive in those days and if I were to have looked through that telescope, would those four insignificantly tiny pinpoints of light have been enough evidence to convince me that the earth was not at the center of the universe? How would *I* have reacted to such a crackpot notion that was contrary to the currently accepted views of the day?

Now it's *your* chance to look through the telescope. Now it's *your* turn to see reality as it really is. What will *you* do?

# Introduction to Reality

It's hard to believe that the small and dusty dirt path on which you are now standing is the famous Grand Imperial Avenue of The Elders, the very highway that had once connected the legendary eight cities of Zendar. Ages ago this region had been a tropical paradise with cool blue lakes and lush forests. Food was plentiful and war was totally unheard of. But those days are far, far in the past — centuries before the era of The Great Catastrophes. Now a different reality exists here, a reality totally foreign to those bygone days of serenity and abundance.

Today all that remains is an arid, lifeless landscape under an unearthly greenish-yellow sky that has no sun or moon — a world that has neither day nor night. Strange rectangular-shaped boulders, some with mysterious markings on them, lie haphazardly scattered over the ground on both sides of the path. Some of the gigantic stones almost seem to have been placed in the form of a pattern, but it's difficult to be sure from your vantage point. Just ahead lie the ruins of the ancient city of Zendar-7. Through the pale reddish mist that surrounds you, you can just make out the remnants of the stone

2    *Shades of Reality*

walls that countless eons ago had surrounded and protected this once-magnificent metropolis.

As you slowly walk down what's left of the path leading to the entrance arch of the city, your ears suddenly become aware of the faint sound of ominous music being played somewhere, but coming from no discernible direction. "Now who on earth could be playing music in a godforsaken place like this?" you mumble to yourself. And then you remember . . . this godforsaken place *isn't* earth. It isn't anything at all like the beloved homeland that you once knew.

Cautiously, you stumble through the frail archway leading into the heart of the ancient city. You pick your way through the crumbling ruins as you slowly head down the main avenue, past the pyramids of Z'adeph and Aristisans, past the statue of Martuus the Great, right up to the base of the Forbidden Temple of the Quellites. And all the while, the music is becoming louder — and louder — and more foreboding.

You are suddenly aware of the object you are holding in your right hand — an object that you have been carrying ever since you arrived on this outermost planet of the Zendar star system. As you slowly raise your hand in front of your eyes, you see what appears to be some kind of high-powered laser pistol being held in a grotesquely deformed stump of a hand — a hand that you've never seen before — a hand that couldn't possibly be yours. And yet, there it is — right at the end of your arm!

Climbing reluctantly up the stairs of the Forbidden Temple you begin to have the uneasy feeling that you are being watched by someone (or some*thing*) from the shadows. Something powerful and evil. Something that even the passing of countless centuries could not kill. And now it's hiding, and waiting . . . for you.

Maybe it's still not too late to turn back. Surely they'll understand. I mean, after all, this *is* your very first mission, and they certainly can't expect a mere rookie like you to . . . .

Then suddenly and without warning, there it is — standing right in front of you and not more than twenty feet away! Drops of

*Introduction to Reality*     3

green slime flow from its hideous scales while insane anger flashes in its blood-red eyes. As the "thing" slowly looks you over, it seems to sneer at you in contempt — as if it knows that you are doomed. For several seconds you stand frozen in terrified fascination, unable to move and unable to think. You stare at the creature's death-ray rifle, which he's holding in his hands. And then you remember the laser pistol in your right hand! You must kill the creature before it kills you!

You begin raising the weapon from your side, but it's too late. A puff of smoke and a flash of blinding light emerge from the creature's rifle. Brilliant colors and lights flash all around and engulf you. A loud clap of thunder fills your ears. And then, as suddenly as it all started, there is nothing but silence . . . and darkness.

You are dead.

"Next time, you're going to have to move a little quicker than that if you ever expect to win the game," warns the attendant as she carefully removes the virtual reality helmet from your head. "But with a little more practice," she says with a smile, " I'm sure you'll eventually get the hang of it."

"But what was that ugly creature who got me?" you ask inquisitively. "It's hard to believe that it was only an image generated by a computer. It acted so real, almost like it was actually alive."

"That was *me*!" shouts a good-looking teenage boy from across the way as he removes his V-R helmet. "You never had a chance! You were 'meat' the minute you started walking up them temple steps!"

"So, it was *you* who 'killed' me, eh?" you say teasingly to your murderer. "Just wait! Next time, you won't be so lucky. I'm a pretty good shot too, y' know!"

It's all a bluff. You never shot a real gun in your life. In fact you know fully well that next time, just like today, you'll be lucky if you can make it through the entire game without accidentally shooting *yourself* with your gun.

4      *Shades of Reality*

"Hey, wait a minute," you suddenly mumble. "What *would* happen if I *did* shoot myself with my own gun?"

The game attendant thinks for a moment. "I'm not really sure *what* would happen," she finally answers. "I think that the computer is programmed to check only for hits on other players in the game, and not on the player doing the shooting. But then nobody has ever really tried it to find out. It would certainly be an interesting experiment!" And then she adds with a smirk, "Someday you'll just have to 'take a shot' at trying it out!"

As you leave the amusement arcade and its fictitious worlds of virtual reality, you are glad that you are finally back into the realm of *real* reality — the reality that contains *real* stuff like blue skies, birds, flowers, trees, and little puppy dogs and kitty cats. Ah, yes, the *real* reality!

And just then a really weird thought flashes through your mind: How do you *know* that this current reality is actually the "real reality"? After all, it was only a few minutes ago that you had experienced a totally *different* "real reality" — a reality located on a far-away planet in the Zendar star system. Is it possible that this *current* reality (the one with the flowers, puppies, kittens, etc.) might also be just another *virtual* reality, a virtual reality in which you have apparently been living for all of your apparent life? Is it possible that one day, when you least expect it, somebody (or something) will suddenly pull off your helmet and shout: "Surprise! You don't really exist! Your whole life has been nothing more than a computer-generated illusion"!

Of course, such an idea is preposterous, right? After all, if you've been wearing a virtual reality helmet on your head all of your life, wouldn't you have been able to see it, or at least feel it by now? And besides, the flickering little low-resolution TV screens inside those helmets are easily distinguishable from real-life vision. And furthermore, when you turn your head while wearing a V-R helmet, there is a slight delay between the time your head starts

*Introduction to Reality*     5

moving and the time the visual display in the helmet responds. And you can probably think of dozens of other "reasons."

But all of these objections are merely technology-based. Granted, the perpetration of such a deception by utilizing only *present-day* virtual reality techniques would be a virtual impossibility (no pun intended). But let's not confine our scope of theoretical possibilities to only those ideas that can be supported by our current meager understanding of possible future technologies.

Let's do a little thought experiment. Imagine a laboratory in another part of the universe (or maybe even in a totally different universe) in which the technological state of the art is millions of years ahead of earth's. On a workbench in this laboratory is a living brain with all kinds of wires, tubes, computers, and other such stuff connected to it. (For the sake of simplicity we will assume that the brain is a "human-type" brain, although such an assumption is not really necessary.) Sensors mounted on the brain intercept signals being sent out, such as, "wiggle the index finger on my right hand." These signals are immediately directed to an ultrasuper computer, which instantaneously generates an ultra-high resolution image of a wiggling finger on a hand. This image is then reformatted into appropriate optic nerve pulses, which are then sent directly into the brain through the optic nerve. What's the result? From the point of view of "the person inside the brain" it appears that he is actually watching himself wiggle "his finger."

It's easy to see that all of the human senses (touch, smell, etc.) could be handled in a similar manner. The ultra high-speed computers could synthesize absolutely *any* stimulus to produce *any* illusion or *any* "reality." An entire virtual lifetime, full of memories of the past and perceptions of the present, could be generated. The brain could be made to view itself as a "person" living in a "real" world, a world containing birds, and flowers, and little puppy dogs and kitty cats. The computers could even create a scenario in which the brain perceives itself as being a person who's reading a *book*. (Think about it!)

6 *Shades of Reality*

And throughout the course of this "lifetime," *there would be absolutely no way for the brain to ever discover the real truth about itself!* Its *perceived* reality would constitute a completely different universe from its *real* reality.

## So, What is Reality?

As our previous discussion illustrated, we can never really know the ultimate answer to this question. It is indeed possible that I may be the only living thing in the universe (assuming that there even *is* a universe!), and that every other person that I've ever seen or met is merely a "prop" in the virtual reality world that has been created for me by some ultrasuper computers. (To paraphrase Descartes: "*I* think, therefore *I* am . . ." but I'm not so sure about *you!*)

I can neither prove nor disprove the premise that "I" may be merely a "brain on a laboratory workbench." But I'm willing to bet that I'm *not*. Otherwise, I might be tempted to try the experiment of shooting myself in what appears to be my head with something that I perceive to be a gun, and then wait to see how the computers would handle it. (But I have a hunch that I wouldn't enjoy the results of *that* experiment *at all!*)

I believe that there is a real physical basis to the perception of reality. When I see a tree, I do not think that it is merely a figment of my imagination (unless I'm suffering from hallucinations), or that it is merely a virtual tree being generated in my brain by some alien computer. When I see a tree, I believe that some entity actually exists, and that entity is the basis for my perception. The entity might actually be a real tree, or it may only be a clever photograph or illusion (such as in a V-R helmet) that fools me into "thinking" that I'm seeing a real tree. But regardless of the mechanism, the cause of my perception ultimately has a real physical explanation. Of course, as we've already discussed, I can never actually prove such a statement. Therefore, I must simply accept that premise on faith.

*Introduction to Reality*    7

## Whose Reality is it?

Clearly, there can be an unlimited number of different *virtual* realities. A computer can be programmed to generate almost any kind of scenario imaginable. But how many different *real* realities can exist? Is it possible that "*my* reality" could be different from "*your* reality"?

It is important to recognize the distinction between *real* reality (sometimes referred to as physical "truth"), and *perceived* reality. Perhaps you have heard the story of the three blind men and the elephant. Once upon a time three blind men were each asked to identify an object by feeling it. (The object was an elephant, but none of the blind men was told that.) The first blind man felt the elephant's trunk and thought that he was touching a hose. The second blind man felt one of the elephant's legs and thought that he was touching the trunk of a tree. The third blind man felt the elephant's tail and thought that he was touching a rope. In this story the three blind men each had a different *perceived* reality (hose, tree trunk, and rope). But the *real* reality (elephant) was the *same* for all three men.

Our perceptions of reality are constantly changing. These perceived realities are sometimes referred to as *paradigms.* In the days of Ptolemy the earth was thought to be the center of the universe. In his paradigm, the earth stood still while the sun, the moon, and all the stars and planets revolved around it. Then Copernicus came along with a different paradigm: Instead of perceiving the *earth* as being at the center of the universe, he imagined that the *sun* was at the center, and the rest of the universe revolved around *it.* But that new view of "reality" also turned out to be wrong. The sun was later found to be part of an even larger structure called the *galaxy.* During the first part of the twentieth century the terms "galaxy" and "universe" were synonymous. But we now "know" (at least we *think* we know) that our galaxy is only one of billions of galaxies in the universe.

8    *Shades of Reality*

Has the *real* reality of the universe actually changed since the time of Ptolemy? Did the earth in those days actually reside at the physical center of the universe, and only just recently move away from that spot? Of course not. The *true nature* of the universe (whatever that true nature may ultimately turn out to be) has not changed. Only our *perceptions* of that ultimate truth have changed. In other words, there is (and always has been) only one *real* reality. Therefore, we will drop the redundant word, "*real*," and from now on we will refer to "*real* reality" as simply, "reality."

## Science

The study of reality goes by a familiar name — it is called *science*. And the primary goal of science is to discover the truths about the entire physical universe. And yet, science is often regarded by the general public as being some kind of esoteric study of *non*-reality!

A few years ago I was out walking with one of my friends who had an interest in science but limited training in the field. As we walked, we started discussing the earth, the solar system, and the Milky Way galaxy. I pointed out that if the entire visible universe were to be scaled down to the size of the planet earth, our Milky Way galaxy would be only about the size of the Goodyear blimp, and our sun would be merely a faint pinpoint of light too small to be seen. I suggested imagining a giant snail crawling along on top of the blimp at the ridiculous rate of one inch per century. Of course no snail could ever move at one inch per century — because, at the current scale of size, one inch per century would be faster than the speed of light!

We talked about the distances between the stars and the existence of black holes, objects so massive that even light cannot escape. We discussed the giant gas and dust clouds, which are still giving rise to the birth of new stars. We walked and talked for several hours. And then, after a while, my friend looked at his watch

*Introduction to Reality* 9

and said that he had completely forgotten about another appointment that he had made.

"It's been fun," he said in parting, "but now I'm afraid it's time for me to get back to reality."

I found his parting comment rather amusing, because *we had just spent the past several hours talking about reality!* And yet, to my friend, "reality" meant nothing more than merely mundane workaday matters. In a complete reversal of perception, the *real* reality was akin to a fantasy or science fiction from *his* point of view!

On other occasions I have heard someone trying to explain some observed phenomenon to a non-technically oriented person. The explainer might say something like, "A lunar eclipse occurs when the moon enters the shadow of the earth." And then the non-technical person would say, "Well, maybe that's the *scientific* explanation," with presumably the assumption that somewhere there exists a different *real* explanation.

But wait a minute. The given answer was not the *scientific* explanation. It was simply *the* explanation. "Scientific" explanations don't describe some kind of *separate* reality. They describe the *one and only* reality. So qualifying the noun, "explanation," with the adjective, "scientific," is redundant.

**Science's Knowledge of Reality**

Science is a dynamic process. The theories and explanations of science are only good insofar as they continue to explain observed reality. If new experiments confirm the theories, the beliefs in the truths of those theories is strengthened. But if an experiment produces results contrary to those explainable by the theories, then the theories must be reformulated to accommodate the new data as well as all of the old data. Any theory that fails to do so does not accurately model physical reality.

As we have already seen, our perceptions of the universe are constantly changing. Sometimes new discoveries are relatively minor

10     *Shades of Reality*

and simply confirm or refine that which we already know (like when we measure the mass of an electron to one more decimal place of accuracy). When this happens we take comfort in thinking that we have moved just that much closer to understanding a part of reality. But then every once in a while a new discovery comes along that is so unexpected and so contrary to what is "known" to be true that it causes a complete *upset* of the prevailing paradigm (like when Galileo first turned a telescope toward the night sky). It's those kinds of experiences that should warn us to always question the credibility of *any* "knowledge" of reality.

The potential uncertainties about what "is" and what "isn't" have led to the introduction of a new way of speaking/writing/thinking known as "E-Prime." The name "E-Prime" (short for "English-Prime") seems to have been coined by David Bourland, but the concept was initially introduced by Alfred Korzybski in *Science and Sanity*. In simple terms, E-Prime replaces the "is" of conventional English with words that more accurately describe our observations or perceptions of reality. We can, in principle, never know what "is." We can only know what we "perceive."

Robert Anton Wilson in his book, *Chaos and Beyond: The Best of Trajectories*, presents several good examples of traditional English phraseology and their corresponding E-Prime constructions:

English:   The electron is a wave.
E-Prime:  The electron appears as a wave when measured with instrument-1.

English:   The electron is a particle.
E-Prime:  The electron appears as a particle when measured with instrument-2.

English:   Beethoven is better than Mozart.
E-Prime:  In my present mixed state of musical education and ignorance, Beethoven seems better to me than Mozart.

*Introduction to Reality*     11

English:    The fetus is a person.

E-Prime:    In my system of metaphysics, the fetus must be classified as a person.

English:    The first man stabbed the second man with a knife.

E-Prime:    The first man appeared to stab the second man with what appeared to me to be a knife.*

The first of each pair of these statements (the ones labeled "English") all assume the notion known as "Aristotelian essentialism," which views the world as being made up of block-like entities with interdwelling "essences." The corresponding E-Prime statements eliminate the "is" of Aristotelian essence and restate each idea in terms of signals that are received and interpreted by an observer.

For example the statement, "The electron is a particle," conveys the erroneous notion that we now know the true interdwelling "essence" of an electron. (And likewise for the conjugate statement, "The electron is a wave.") But in the Aristotelian framework, if A "*is*" B then A cannot "*be*" something else substantially different from B. And so we end up with what appears to be a contradiction.

However, when expressed in terms that more accurately reflect the basis for our knowledge and/or inferences, the statement, "The electron appears to be a wave when measured one way" and the statement, "The electron appears to be a particle when measured another way" do *not* contradict each other. Instead, they merely represent two different observations of the same physical reality.

**Facts vs. Opinions**

Webster's Collegiate Dictionary defines "opinion" as: "belief stronger than impression and less strong than positive knowledge."

---

*Mr. Wilson could have taken this last application of E-Prime even further: "The first entity which I perceived to be a man appeared to stab another entity, which I also perceived to be a man, with a third entity which appeared to me to be a knife."

12      *Shades of Reality*

But as we have already pointed out, we can never have *positive knowledge* about *anything* in physical reality. Therefore, any statement about physical reality expresses nothing more than an opinion. For example, it is my *opinion* that the earth rotates on its axis. But there always remains the possibility that, in a few thousand years or so, scientists may discover that even *that* is not true (in the light of some yet-to-be proposed paradigm about the then-to-be "true" nature of the space-time continuum).

However, there are statements that *do* represent facts. For example the statement "two plus two equals four" is a *fact*. It is not merely my *opinion* that "two plus two equals four." Factual statements of this type are referred to as *logical truths*. (We will discuss the concept of "truth" further in Chapter Four.)

It might be conceivable that your old high school science teacher might phone you someday and tell you that the earth actually *doesn't* rotate. And if that were to happen, you *could* accept the fact that you've been wrong all this time. But if your old math teacher were to phone you and say that he lied when he taught you that 2 + 2 equals 4, you *wouldn't* be able to buy it. Because you already *know* that 2 + 2 can't be anything else *but* 4. Such truths do not require that we take someone else's word for them, nor do they depend upon our perceptions of physical reality.

## Science vs. Religion

But what about God, and the Devil, and Guardian Angels? What about places like Heaven and Hell? Do any of these things have an existence in physical reality? You will always be able to find closed-minded religious fanatics who claim to have all the answers to these kinds of questions (because Jesus told them, or because they "know in their hearts" that such and such is true). And, on the other side of the coin, atheists with equal but opposite zeal will make authoritative counterclaims of their own.

*Introduction to Reality*　　13

We will continue discussing some of these religious questions later on in this book. But for now, let me just state the obvious: nobody *knows* if God exists. However, we can say this much: If God *does* exist, then He (or She, or It) must exist in *reality*. Otherwise, God would be merely a *virtual* being who exists only in your mind and consequently would be no more real than a fantasy or a dream. But if God *does* exist in reality, then the study of God must necessarily be a part of that discipline which studies reality — namely *science!*

Perhaps someday in the future, science will either prove or disprove the existence of God. If that time should ever come when all of reality becomes known and understood (don't hold your breath!), and if God *does* truly exist in reality, then we will have found Him. But whatever the final outcome turns out to be, we will have to accept it. Because there is only one ultimate reality. And that reality will be whatever it *is*.

# Chapter Zero

# Consistency and Correctness

The earth takes about 365¼ days to make one complete revolution around the sun. (According to a 1996 survey conducted by the National Science Foundation, half of the American public was unaware of this fact!) This period of time (which we call a *year*) is divided into four seasons: spring, summer, autumn, and winter.

The start and end of each season is defined in terms of the angle between the earth's spin axis and an imaginary line from the center of the earth to the center of the sun. When this angle reaches its minimum value (about 66.5 degrees) we call it the *summer solstice*, and that day marks the beginning of summer (around June 21st). Summer continues until the angle between the earth's spin axis and the earth-sun line reaches 90 degrees (the *autumnal equinox*), at which time summer ends and autumn begins (around September 21st). The *winter solstice* occurs (around December 21st) when the angle reaches its maximum value (about 113.5 degrees). This marks the end of autumn and the beginning of winter. When the angle returns to 90 degrees (the *vernal equinox*), winter ends and spring begins (around March 21st). And when the angle once

*Consistency and Correctness*     15

again returns to its minimum value, spring ends and summer begins, and the cycle of the seasons is complete.

The seasons of the year are therefore determined by an aspect of *physical reality*, namely the angle between the earth's spin axis and the earth-sun line. If, for some reason, a question were to arise as to which season it currently is, all you would have to do is measure the angle between the earth-sun line and the earth's spin axis. From that angle you could easily determine the current season.

### Is Today Wednesday?

But now consider a slightly different question: What *day of the week* is today? (Let's assume that today is Wednesday.) How do you *know* that today is Wednesday? What physical measurement can you perform that will verify that today is actually Wednesday and not some other day of the week, like maybe Saturday? (No, asking someone else what day of the week they think it is does *not* constitute performing a physical measurement! Besides, how would you know whether or not they're right? Nor will looking at a calendar be acceptable, because it might be possible that all of our calendars are wrong too!)

Unlike the seasons of the year, there is no way to determine physically what the current day of the week really is. (There is nothing in physical reality that we can associate with "Wednesday-ness.") The days of the week (and even the notion of a "week," itself) are man-made concepts. That we call today "Wednesday" is therefore quite arbitrary. It could just as easily have been called "Saturday."

So, if the days of the week are completely arbitrary, then wouldn't it be just as correct to call today "Saturday" as it is to call it "Wednesday"? In fact if I were to go out and tell everyone that today *is* Saturday, and if they were to tell me that I'm wrong — it's only *Wednesday* — would their refutation have any real validity? Why would *their* claim of *Wednesday* be any more correct than *my* claim of *Saturday*?

16     *Shades of Reality*

It's true that the names of the days of the week have no physical significance and, as such, are arbitrarily named. (For example, the name "*Sunday*" has nothing to do with the position of the sun.) Even the chronological order of the days of the week is arbitrary. For example, Monday *could* have followed Thursday, which in turn *could* have followed Saturday, etc., if we had so chosen. But we *didn't*. So even though the days of the week may have been *initially* specified in a completely arbitrary manner, once those names and their chronological sequence were specified, they became established *for all time*.

Therefore, today *is* Wednesday. Why? Only because yesterday was Tuesday, and the rule is that Wednesday always follows Tuesday.

When dealing with man-made truths about reality (such as the days of the week), adherence to an established pattern is the *only* way to resolve issues of correctness. Therefore,

**Consistency determines the correctness of man-made "truths."**

It is therefore incorrect to call today "Saturday," simply because doing so would violate the pattern that we've established for naming the days of the week. (Saturday does *not* follow Tuesday.) The only way to be consistent with our established convention for naming the days of the week is to call today "Wednesday."

But let's suppose that we all got together and *agreed* to let today, and only today, be an exception. Suppose we all agreed to call today "Saturday" instead of "Wednesday." But starting tomorrow (Thursday) we would all once again resume calling the days by their "correct" names. Then wouldn't today actually "be" Saturday?

There are some philosophers who will argue "yes." Since the days of the week are our own creation, we can call them whatever we want to. After all they're only words, and a word can mean whatever we choose it to mean.

In Lewis Carroll's *Alice Through The Looking Glass,* Humpty Dumpty says to Alice:

*Consistency and Correctness*     **17**

">. . .There are three hundred and sixty-four days when you might get unbirthday presents —"

"Certainly," said Alice.

"And only *one* for birthday presents, you know. There's glory for you!"

"I don't know what you mean by 'glory,'" Alice said.

Humpty Dumpty smiled contemptuously. "Of course you don't — till I tell you. I meant 'there's a nice knock-down argument for you!'"

"But 'glory' doesn't mean 'a nice knock-down argument,'" Alice objected.

"When *I* use a word," Humpty Dumpty said, in rather a scornful tone, "it means just what I choose it to mean — neither more nor less."

"The question is," said Alice, "whether you *can* make words mean so many different things."

"The question is," said Humpty Dumpty, "which is to be master — that's all."

(I wonder if Humpty Dumpty is responsible for the popular misuse of the word "organic." There was a time when "organic" simply meant "composed of carbon compounds." Now its meaning seems to have been changed to: "grown without pesticides"!)

There is nothing intrinsically special about the names of the days of the week themselves. Instead of assigning each day a name like "Saturday" (Saturn's day), "Sunday" (the sun's day), "Monday" (the moon's day), and so on, we could just as easily have given each day of the week a different name like "Jovday" (Jupiter's day), "Venday" (Venus' day), etc. Or we might have even given each day a totally meaningless name like "Krepstin," "Shlugsty," "Dorkelding," or anything else we might have come up with. Insofar as that part of the naming process goes, we are free to do whatever we choose.

But while we may be free to assign and reassign absolute names to entities (such as days of the week), we are *not* completely at liberty to assign and reassign their interrelationships in a willy-nilly fashion. For example if we were to rename the days of the week, and if we were to define "Shlugsty" as being the day follow-

18     *Shades of Reality*

ing "Krepstin," then "Dorkelding" (a completely separate day from "Shlugsty") could *not* also be defined as being the day following "Krepstin" or else we would have a conflict — there would be an *inconsistency* in our system.

*Once a consistent interrelationship between a group of entities has been established, that interrelationship must either remain consistent, or else the entire system of interrelationships must be redefined in such a way as to produce a new consistency.*

So there are some definite restrictions imposed on us whenever we attempt to define or redefine man-made "truths." We are not always completely at liberty to arbitrarily pick and choose the meanings and associations of all the words that we use. (Sorry about that, Mr. Dumpty!)

Getting back to our hypothetical question, if everybody agreed to call today "Saturday" would it really *be* Saturday? My answer is *no*, it would still be Wednesday. (We would all just be "pretending" that it's Saturday, either out of conformity or out of ignorance.)

Consistency is a very powerful concept — it has almost a kind of mathematical rigor to it. In fact consistency is the "glue" which holds mathematics together. If an inconsistency were ever to be discovered in mathematics, the entire system of mathematics would collapse. (We'll discuss this further in Chapter Five when we talk about Fallacy & Paradox.) An inconsistent statement cannot be "declared" to be a "truth" any more than the value of $2 + 2$ can be "declared" to be equal to 5, or that the value of *pi* can be "declared" to be exactly equal to 3.

### Patterns of Consistency

We've all seen puzzle questions in which we are given a sequence of numbers, and we are asked to determine the next number in the sequence. For example, given the sequence:

$$11, 13, 15, 17, 19, 21, 23, 25, 27, \_\_$$

*Consistency and Correctness*     **19**

what number would come next? Obviously the sequence represents the list of double-digit odd numbers, so the correct answer would be 29.

In solving a puzzle of this form you must first try to detect a pattern of consistency between the items in the sequence. Once you determine a pattern it usually becomes a trivial matter to specify the next item in the sequence.

But now try to determine the number which comes next in the following sequence:

$$1, 2, 4, \_\_$$

Now the correct answer is not so obvious because there is much less information to work with. In fact the lack of information in this problem results in the existence of *many* correct answers.

For example, the sequence represents the powers of two ($2^0$, $2^1, 2^2, 2^3, \ldots$ ). Therefore a correct answer would be 8.

On the other hand, the sequence represents those integers that are not a multiple of three (1, 2, 4, 5, 7, 8, 10, ... ). So a correct answer in this case would be 5.

In fact it's easy to show (not only for this particular problem, but for all of these types of sequence puzzles in general) that *any* number can be the "correct" answer! First construct a polynomial whose roots are the numbers in the given sequence:

$$P(x) = (x - 1)(x - 2)(x - 4)$$

Then pick any number (we'll choose 7) and multiply the polynomial by $(x - 7)$ to create a new polynomial:

$$Q(x) = (x - 7) P(x)$$
$$= (x - 1)(x - 2)(x - 4)(x - 7)$$

You can now justifiably argue that the "correct" answer (to the problem of trying to determine the next number in the sequence: 1, 2, 4, ... ) is therefore 7, because the numbers 1, 2, 4, and 7 all represent the roots of the polynomial, $Q(x)$.

20    *Shades of Reality*

Correctness is therefore not something which is necessarily unique. There can be more than one correct solution to any problem. The only requirement for a solution to be correct is that it be consistent with the given data. However, some correct solutions may represent better solutions than others.

## Occam's Razor

In science, when two different hypotheses (one simple and one more complicated) can both be used equally well to explain an observed phenomenon, the simpler hypothesis is adopted as representing the correct explanation. This practice is commonly referred to as using *Occam's razor* and is based on our empirical experience that nature (i.e., physical reality) actually *does* appear to have a fundamental simplicity to it.

Even though the concept of consistency is not based on a *physical* reality, we can nevertheless invoke the spirit of Occam's razor to determine the relative correctness of two or more competing solutions to a problem. In this case, Occam's razor will not be used to completely eliminate solutions by declaring them to be totally "incorrect." Instead, it will merely declare some of the solutions to be less *desirable* (or "less correct") than others.

In our first puzzle (the sequence: 11, 13, 15, etc.) we could also have justified *any* number as being the next correct number, just like we did in the second puzzle. But when confronted with the choice of having to accept between either justifying our answer as being one of the roots of a complicated $10^{th}$ degree polynomial, or more simply as being the next odd number in the sequence, Occam's razor tells us that the latter choice represents the more desirable answer.

Returning once again to the question about whether or not today would actually be Saturday (if we all simply declared it to be so), Occam's razor can guide us in determining that answer as well. If today *would* really be Saturday, then we would have to regard

*Consistency and Correctness*     21

today as being an *exception* to our rule that Wednesday *always* follows Tuesday (since yesterday really *was* Tuesday). On the other hand if today would really be Wednesday (like it normally would have been), then there would *not* have to be any exceptions to the rule that Wednesday *always* follows Tuesday. Since *consistent* rules (ones without exceptions) are cleaner and simpler than *inconsistent* rules (ones with messy exceptions), Occam's razor confirms that today would indeed still be Wednesday.

Consistency is a powerful tool. Besides allowing us to determine the correct day of the week, the principle of consistency can be used to determine the correctness (or incorrectness) of many other commonly accepted conventions currently used in everyday life.

**A Quickie Question:**

If a person who is addicted to alcohol is referred to as being an alcoholic, then how should we refer to a person who is addicted to work? (I'll give the answer at the end of this chapter.)

**Specifying Calendar Dates**

In 1969 Neil Armstrong became the first man to walk on the moon. That event occurred on July 20$^{th}$ of that year. Most of us would probably express that date as:

July 20, 1969

or, using only numbers, as:

7/20/69

But is this the *correct* form in which to specify dates? Is the order in which the numbers are specified (the month, followed by the day, followed by the year) consistent with how we write numbers in general?

Let's look, for example, at a number like "three hundred fifty-

22    *Shades of Reality*

two." How would we express that number using numerical digits instead of words? The arbitrarily established convention that we've adopted is to first write down the *most significant* digit (the one that represents the largest portion of the number, in this case the 3, since it represents "hundreds"), followed to the right by the *next most significant* digit (in this case the 5, since it represents "tens"), followed to the right by the *least significant* digit (in this case the 2, since it represents "ones"). Therefore the number would look like this:

**352**

As an aside, the fact that we write the digits in this particular order is *completely arbitrary*. We could have just as easily adopted some other convention, such as writing the same digits from *right* to *left* instead (i.e., 253). And, had we chosen to write all of our numbers that way, then that convention would have been just as "correct" as the "left-to-right" method that we actually use. (Of course 253 would then *not* indicate "two hundred fifty-three.")

The left-to-right convention is also the way we express clock time. For example "four twenty-seven and fifty-one seconds" would be expressed by first writing the most significant portion (the hours), followed to the right by the next most significant portion (the minutes), followed to the right by the least significant portion (the seconds). Using colons to delimit each portion, the time would therefore be written as:

**4:27:51**

So then why do we express calendar time by writing the *most significant* portion (the year) in the right-most position? The correct (i.e., consistent) way to write a date is to first write the most significant portion (the year), followed to the right by the next significant portion (the month), followed to the right by the least significant portion (the day). Therefore the correct way to express the date of the first lunar landing is:

**1969 July 20**

*Consistency and Correctness*     23

or, using only numbers, as:

**69/7/20**

In fact, since clocks and calendars both indicate quantities of "time," the most consistent way of specifying time in general would be to combine those two separate concepts into one single concept. Any point in time could then be expressed in the single form:

**year : month : day : hour : minute : second**

where we would no longer require a separate delimiter (such as a "/") to be used only for the "date" portion.

## Counting

Surely everyone knows how to count . . . or at least they *think* that they do. Let's see if you know the correct way to count. I would like for you to count *out loud* the number of x's contained inside the parentheses below:

( x x x x x )

No, I don't want you to just give the answer, "five." I want you to actually *count* each item.

Did you say: "One . . . two . . . three . . . four . . . five"? Is that what you think of as being the correct way to count? OK then, try counting (out loud again) the number of x's contained inside *these* parentheses:

(     )

No, I don't want you to just give me the answer: "There aren't any." I want you to actually *count* the items.

What's the matter? Having problems? And I thought you said that you knew how to count!

The *correct* way to count is *not* to start with *one*, but with *zero*. If you start counting with *one*, you are automatically making

## 24  *Shades of Reality*

the unwarranted assumption that there actually *is* at least one item to be counted. (If you really want to make such groundless a priori assumptions about the number of items that you will be counting, then you might as well always start counting with some even *higher* number, like maybe *three*. Then you can simply skip over to the third item and begin your counting from there!)

To count *correctly* you need to first perform a very simple "initialization" step. Before you even look at the items to be counted, you merely say "zero." In mathematical terms this step can be thought of as counting the *null set*, an empty set that exists in *every* collection of items. You then look for the first item (if there is one) and continue counting from there.

Therefore the correct way to count the first collection of x's would be:

**"Zero . . . one . . . two . . . three . . . four . . . five"**

and the correct way to count the second "collection" would be:

**"Zero"**

By counting in this manner you can consistently count any number of items (including *no* items) without having to treat the case of "nothing to count" as a special case. (Remember that Occam's razor abhors rules that require exceptions and special cases.)

Failure to acknowledge zero as the first step in counting has led to the establishment of many awkward conventions. For example the new millennium begins (or began, depending on when you read this) with the year 2001, and not with 2000 (as the general population seems to think). And the reason, of course, is because there was no year numbered "zero AD."

As another example of awkwardness, consider the popular question: "On a scale from *one* to ten how would you rate such and such"? Then, even though you absolutely *hate* such and such, you are still required to give it at least *one* point!

*Consistency and Correctness*     25

The idea of specifying a "zero[th] step" (i.e., an initialization step) is fundamental to almost every activity, especially those of an iterative nature. You cannot, in general, just "jump into the loop" until you first make some kind of initial preparation. (Even a book sometimes needs to prepare its readers by presenting them with certain background material that may be somewhat removed from its main theme. Therefore its chapter numbers might not necessarily begin with "one.")

### Is 12 O'clock Noon AM or PM?

The letters AM and PM are abbreviations for the Latin expressions "*ante meridiem*" and "*post meridiem*," respectively. (*Ante* and *post* are Latin for "before" and "after," respectively. *Meridiem* is the Latin word for "meridian," the imaginary great circle on the celestial sphere, which passes through the point in the sky directly overhead, and through the point on the horizon directly south of the observer.) Every day the sun spends essentially half of its time to the east of the meridian (i.e., *ante meridiem*), and half of its time to the west (*post meridiem*). And the crossover point (the middle of the daylight portion of the day) defines *local noon*, the time when the sun reaches its highest point above the horizon.

Because the meridian is defined in terms of an observer, the exact time at which local noon occurs depends on where the particular observer is located. Therefore, local noon seldom (if ever) occurs exactly at "clock-time" noon (i.e., twelve o'clock). So if one were to interpret the meanings of AM and PM literally, then the exact time at which "AM becomes PM" would not be at 12 o'clock, but would instead occur at different times for observers at different locations.

Even adopting the concept of "standard meridians" (i.e., 24 fixed meridians, one for each of the time zones) would not solve the problem because the sun does not make meridian crossings (of *any* meridian) in exactly 24 hour intervals. Since the orbit of the earth

26    *Shades of Reality*

around the sun is not a perfect circle, the times of the sun's meridian crossings slowly change from day to day. Over the course of a year, this daily drift (known as the "equation of time") can amount to as much as about plus or minus 18 minutes. (On globes of the earth the equation of time is sometimes represented graphically as an *analemma*, a skinny "figure-eight" shape that usually gets printed somewhere around the area of the Pacific Ocean.) Therefore, even measured relative to a standard meridian, the time at which "AM becomes PM" would *still* not be constant.

And to make matters even worse, six months out of the year are represented by Daylight Savings Time (when the sun actually crosses the meridian an hour *later* than our clocks would otherwise indicate). Should we therefore refer to the noon hour as being PM during the winter, but AM during the summer?

When specifying clock times it is clearly impractical to try to interpret the meanings of AM and PM in their literal senses. Instead, we should interpret AM as simply being a reference to the *first half of the day*, and PM as being a reference to the *second half of the day*. Therefore, specifying a time like 7:45 AM simply means that 7 hours and 45 minutes of time have elapsed since the start of the *first* half of the day (i.e., since midnight). Similarly, specifying a time like 4:15 PM means that 4 hours and 15 minutes of time have elapsed since the start of the *second* half of the day (i.e., since noon).

We can now quite easily determine the answer to our question about whether 12:00 noon should be designated as AM or PM. (And our discussion pertains not only to the *instant* of noon, but to the *entire noon hour*.)

Let's first start with 2 o'clock in the afternoon. Should 2 o'clock in the afternoon be designated as AM or PM? Answer: PM. Why? Because 2:00 PM means that 2 hours of time have elapsed since the start of the second half of the day (i.e., since noon).

Now let's back up an hour, to 1 o'clock. Should 1 o'clock in the afternoon be designated as AM or PM? Answer: PM. Why?

*Consistency and Correctness*     27

Because 1:00 PM means that 1 hour of time has elapsed since the start of the second half of the day (i.e., since noon).

Now let's back up one more hour, to noon. Should 12:00 noon be designated as AM or PM? Answer: AM. Why? Because 12:00 AM means that 12 hours of time have elapsed since the start of the *first* half of the day (i.e., since *midnight*). (To refer to noon as being 12:00 PM would be tantamount to making the clearly absurd claim that noon occurs 12 hours *later than* noon!) Therefore,

**12:00 AM is actually *Noon***

and

**12:00 PM is actually *Midnight*.**

(No, 12:01 in the afternoon is not PM *either*. It doesn't become PM until one o'clock.)

"B-b-but . . ." you protest, "That's just the *opposite* of the way that everybody does it. We've defined *noon* as being 12:00 <u>PM</u>, and *midnight* as being 12:00 <u>AM</u>."

"I'm sorry, but they were defined incorrectly," is my reply. And it's not just my *opinion* that they're incorrect. They *are* incorrect. Referring to noon as 12:00 PM (and to midnight as 12:00 AM) is inconsistent. And inconsistencies cannot be "declared" to be *truths*. And even if everybody *agrees* to call noon 12:00 PM, that still won't make it so. (Recall our prior discussion about everybody agreeing to call today Saturday when it's really only Wednesday.)

Still, there remains a nagging compulsion in the back of your mind. You're thinking: "If it's even as little as a fraction of a second into the afternoon, then it's just somehow *got to be* PM. After all, PM *refers* to the afternoon, doesn't it? So why *can't* we legitimately use PM?"

The answer is: **We *can*!** (But if we do, then we can no longer refer to the time as being <u>12</u> o'clock.) Let me explain:

As we have already indicated, whenever we express a time in terms of PM hours, we are specifying (or *counting*) the number of

28    *Shades of Reality*

hours (and minutes and seconds) that have elapsed since noon. So if we want to express noon *itself* as a PM time, then all we have to do is *count* (out loud, if you please!) the number of hours between noon and *itself.*

Yes, *"ZERO!"*

Therefore:

**Noon can be expressed as *Zero* o'clock PM**

And of course, by identical reasoning:

**Midnight can be expressed as *Zero* o'clock AM**

What? You say that your clock doesn't *have* a zero on it? Well, that's easy enough to fix. Just scrape off the twelve (which never should have been put there in the first place) and paste on a zero instead! After all, who in their right mind would ever want to suggest that we should begin *counting* things (such as the hours of a new day) by starting with — *twelve*!

(When I presented this information on one of my radio shows several years ago, a listener came down to the station the next day and presented me with just such a clock on which he had carefully replaced the twelve with a zero! That clock is still mounted on the wall in the lobby at KSCO.)


**Unrestricted Time**

Now that we've opened the door to the concept that clock hours do not have to be restricted to the range 1 through 12, let's carry that idea a little further.

When we count things (be they apples, marbles, or whatever), there is no restriction on us that says we must *stop* counting when we reach *twelve*. The same holds true for hours. (In fact we often *do* use expressions such as "48 hours" in our everyday speech.) Therefore, we can count *past* 12 AM and legitimately refer to the succeeding times as being 13 AM, 14 AM, etc. (This should come as no surprise to anybody who is familiar with "military" time.)

*Consistency and Correctness*     29

But there's no reason why we can't also extend this concept to the PM hours as well. In this case, 13 PM, 14 PM, etc. are equivalent to 1 AM, 2 AM, etc. *of the following day*. Therefore:

1 PM on October 1st
13 AM on October 1st
25 PM on September 30th
37 AM on September 30th
49 PM on September 29th
etc.

all refer to exactly the same instant of time. (For example the fifth item on the above list, 49 PM on September 29th, simply indicates the point in time that occurs 49 hours after the noon of September 29th.) Furthermore, all of these representations are *correct* ways of expressing that same instant in time, because all of the representations are consistent.

There is also no need to limit ourselves to only *positive* numbers. For example we can refer to 11 AM as being –1 PM, 10 AM as being –2 PM, etc. These times may look funny and they may be awkward to use. But it is not incorrect to specify them, if we so choose.

When viewing time in this unrestricted way, the true significance of "AM" and "PM" becomes readily apparent. It is no longer meaningful to simply declare that a given point in time, such as sunset, occurs "in the PM hours." Because:

**Any point in time can be *either* AM *or* PM, depending on the *number* that is placed in front of those letters.**

The terms "AM" and "PM" are simply *reference indicators* that allow you to specify which "zero point in time" you have chosen to use.

### Unrestricted Dates

As we have already mentioned, calendar dates are just another

30    *Shades of Reality*

expression of time. However, instead of having only *two* reference points (AM or PM) to choose from, we now have *twelve* (January, February, etc.). Therefore, just as in the case of clock time, we can express calendar time in an unrestricted fashion. (Dates need not be restricted to the "actual" number of days in the month.)

For example, my birthday (September 2nd) could also be expressed as: August 33rd, October 28th, etc. Each expression represents a consistent (and therefore correct) way of designating the same actual day.

## The English Language

No discussion about consistency and inconsistency would be complete without at least mentioning the English language with all of its inconsistencies and exceptions to rules. To delve into all of its inconsistencies, however, would make this chapter longer than the entire rest of the book! But the messy state of the language can probably be best summed up and illustrated by the old joke that the word "fish" could have been spelled as "g-h-o-t-i" (*gh* as in the word "lau*gh*," *o* as in the word "w*o*men," and *ti* as in the word "mo-*ti*on")!

## Answer to Quickie Question:

A person addicted to *work* would properly (i.e., consistently) be referred to as being a *workic* (not a work*aholic*). The term "workaholic" would properly refer to a person who is addicted to "workahol" (whatever *that* is!)

# Part One

# The Foundations of the Fuzzy Paradigm

# Chapter One

# The Smoothness Principle

The beach is almost deserted as the day comes to an end. The last of the sun worshipers are packing up their beach blankets and bottles of suntan lotion and are heading for their parked cars. Soon there will be nobody here except you and a few seagulls who frantically fight over the few remaining scraps of discarded sandwiches and potato chips left behind by the departing throng.

As the sun slowly sinks below the clouds on the western horizon, the sky gradually takes on a new set of colors — delicate shades of red, orange, and purple — which gently nudge away the blue in preparation for the coming of the night. Even now you can just about begin to make out one or two stars, and then a few more, and soon even more still. Meanwhile, as you walk along the edge of the water, the sky to the west still continues to glow with the soft golden-red luster of twilight.

The sea breeze has started to become quite cool now, and you wish that you had had the foresight to bring your jacket with you. And since it's getting harder and harder to see where you're walking, you decide that it's time for you to start heading back home.

*The Smoothness Principle*    **33**

The walk back to your house is pleasant but uneventful, and you soon find yourself standing next to the steps of your front porch. As you glance upward, you see thousands of tiny diamonds twinkling in the night sky, and you contemplate the idea that some of those tiny lights are actually even bigger and brighter than our own sun.

## A "Simple" Question

I hope that you enjoyed your little trip to the beach and that you didn't get too sunburned. But now I would like to ask you something: When you left home this morning to go to the beach, it was light outside. But by the time you got back to your house, it was already dark. Now, we all know the difference between light and dark. They each represent totally opposite concepts. (In fact the two concepts are about as different from each other as *night* and *day*!) So you shouldn't have any trouble answering the following little question: **When did the sky become dark?**

"It became dark after the sun went down," is probably the answer that you would give. "Everybody knows that!" you say.

True, but could you please be a little bit more specific? How *much* after? One second? One minute? One hour? I want to know the exact *instant* at which the daylight ended — the moment when "not dark" turned into "dark."

## Another "Simple" Question

If that question was too tough for you, then let's try a different one (but also about the same beach): ***Where* is the boundary line between the beach and the ocean?**

"Well, *that's* an easy one," you say. "The ocean is the part that has the water, and the beach is the part that has the sand. And where they meet, well, that defines the boundary line."

OK, but once again, I'm looking for a more *exact* answer. For example, how about the sand that is *wet*? Should it be classified as

## 34 Shades of Reality

being part of the ocean because it has water on it, or should it be classified as being part of the beach? And how wet or dry does the sand have to become before it changes classification? Furthermore, consider water that has washed up onto the beach and formed into little pools. Should such pools be classified as being part of the *ocean*, or part of the *beach*?

By now you are probably thinking to yourself: "Who cares? These kinds of questions are completely trite and meaningless. I've got better things to do with my time than to sit around thinking about silly things like finding the exact time of day when the sky gets dark"! And to some extent you're right! The actual answers to the questions (if answers even exist) are totally irrelevant. For example, suppose I were to say to you: "The correct answer to the question (about the sky getting dark) is exactly 27.3 seconds past 6:48 PM." (That's *not* the answer, but let's pretend that it is.) Of what use would that particular piece of information be?

My sole purpose in asking the questions is to point out an extremely important (but seldom recognized) aspect of reality, which I call the **smoothness principle:**

### Everything in physical reality occurs smoothly.

What the smoothness principle says is that physical changes do not occur instantaneously at some *point* in time (Figure 1.1). Instead, all changes take place over a *period* of time, and they take place in a continuous way (Figure 1.2). In other words, the mathematical concept of a *step function* does not exist in physical reality.

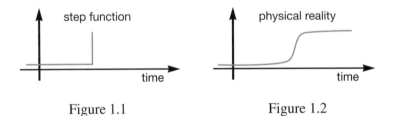

Figure 1.1       Figure 1.2

*The Smoothness Principle*     35

As another example of the smoothness principle, imagine that you are holding one end of a horizontal ten-foot steel pole and the other end is inside a furnace. Your end of the pole may still be quite cool even though the other end of the pole is red hot. Yet there is no precise location along the pole where the temperature changes from hot to cool.

Or consider the metamorphosis of a tadpole into a frog. There is no point in time at which anyone can meaningfully say, "One second ago it was still only a tadpole, but *now* it is definitely a frog."

The smoothness principle may come as a surprise to many readers, and they are undoubtedly already constructing a mental list of "Oh yeah?—what-abouts." Let me see if I can anticipate some of them.

### "Oh yeah? What about switching on a lightbulb?"

When electricity flows through the filament of a lightbulb, the filament requires a finite amount of time to heat up. The bulb does not just light up "all of a sudden."

Likewise, turning off a lightbulb doesn't instantaneously cause the bulb to become dark. It is easy to verify this for yourself, if you use a clear (not frosted) bulb in which you can see the filament. Close your eyes while the bulb is on. And then, just as you turn the bulb off, quickly open your eyes. You can actually see the filament fading out. In fact it still continues to emit light even long after it *appears* to have reached its "off" state. But this light is in the infrared portion of the spectrum, and the human eye cannot see it.

### "Oh yeah? What about the instant when a stick of dynamite explodes?"

An explosion is nothing more than an example of combustion, except that it takes place very quickly. Molecules of the explosive combine with molecules of the oxidant and release thermal energy,

## 36    *Shades of Reality*

which in turn, causes other molecules to combine. But it requires a finite amount of time for the individual molecules to interact with each other, so the combustion does not occur all at once. (And even if it did, the expanding ball of hot gas has limits on how fast it can expand.)

By using high-speed photography, even the flight of a bullet (which is nothing more than the result of a tiny explosion of gunpowder) can be continuously observed.

### "Oh yeah? What about the instant when two billiard balls collide?"

It might seem intuitive to define a "collision" as being the exact instant in time when any atom of one of the balls just touches any atom of the other ball. And so the two balls should abruptly change from a state of *not-touching* to a state of *touching* at some precise moment.

The flaws in this intuitive definition are that it incorrectly assumes that atoms are objects that have well-defined boundaries, and that the individual atoms of each ball are totally motionless with respect to its neighboring atoms. We know that all atoms are in constant motion because of thermal energy. And quantum theory tells us that their precise locations are slightly "smeared out" (the Heisenberg uncertainty principle). As the two atoms approach each other, they begin to "feel" each other's presence gradually. Therefore, even billiard balls have an extremely slight degree of smoothness to their collisions.

### "Oh yeah? What about the instant when 'Monday' becomes 'Tuesday'?"

The smoothness principle only applies to *physical* events. Terms like "Monday" and "Tuesday" are *man-made concepts* and, as such, can take on whatever attributes we wish to assign them.

*The Smoothness Principle*     37

Therefore the day of the week changes "instantly" simply because we *say* it does!

It might seem as if I'm being a little nitpicky in some of my justifications, but then I have to be. Because reality doesn't merely "go away" just because things may have gotten too small or too fast for our eyes to see. Still, we like to *pretend* that it does, so that we can make our world view simpler. "For all practical purposes," is the phrase we like to use. But, in so pretending, it is important not to lose sight of the distinction between the *practicality* and the *reality*.

**The Mismatch Problem**

That the smoothness principle may have initially struck you as somewhat surprising, is symptomatic of a phenomenon sometimes referred to as the mismatch problem — *reality is gray, but in our minds the world is black and white*. A lightbulb is either on, or it's off. Each person in our society is either an adult, or else they're a minor. A window is either open, or it's closed. A body of water is either a lake, or it isn't a lake. If something isn't *all*, then it's *nothing*.

In reality, vague boundaries exist between things and not things — between day and not day — between lakes and not lakes. At what point does "dry" become "damp," and when does "damp" become "wet"? How does one differentiate between very wet ground and a small puddle of water? What's the difference between a very large puddle and a small pond? What distinguishes a large pond from a small lake? Minnesota claims to be the land of 10,000 lakes. Clearly this is an exaggerated estimate. But if somebody were to try to count them, would the actual number of lakes in Minnesota turn out to be an *even* number or an *odd* number?

When does the battery in a flashlight have to be replaced? At what precise instant does the light become dim enough to justify referring to the battery as no longer being "good." A battery starts to become "bad" the first moment you use it. And even a so-called

38     *Shades of Reality*

"dead" battery usually has at least a tiny amount of electricity still in it.

Since transitions in the real world don't happen at *points*, questions like: "At what point did the sky get dark?" are semantically meaningless and self-contradictory (like asking about the distinct smell of an odorless gas, or asking about what it feels like to be dead). Furthermore, since there is no distinct boundary line for the transition, it is difficult to determine if certain specific points in time should be classified as being in the category called "day" or the category called "night." However, at any point in time, the question: "Is it dark yet?" *does* have a meaningful answer! I will explain what I mean later in the book.

**The Fuzzy Principle**

In his book, *Fuzzy Thinking* (pages 18-19), Bart Kosko defines what he calls the "Fuzzy Principle: *Everything* is a matter of degree." However, he acknowledges that things from the world of mathematics are *not* fuzzy. An expression like, "Two plus two equals four," is 100 percent true. But when we move out of the artificial world of math, fuzziness reigns. Kosko writes:

"Fuzziness has a formal name in science: multivalence. The opposite of fuzziness is bivalence or two-valuedness, two ways to answer each question, true or false, 1 or 0. Fuzziness means multivalence. It means three or more options, perhaps an infinite spectrum of options, instead of just two extremes. It means analog instead of binary, infinite shades of gray between black and white. It means all that the trial lawyer or judge tries to rule out when she says, 'Answer just yes or no.'"

What Kosko is saying is that fuzziness increases as the valence increases. The more options there are (i.e., the more *multi* the multivalence is), the greater the degree of fuzziness. (Yes, even fuzziness comes in degrees!) But it is incorrect to say that bivalence is the *opposite* of fuzziness, and that fuzziness "means *three* or

*The Smoothness Principle*     39

more options." (*Non*-fuzzy does not suddenly become *fuzzy* at the three-option boundary line!)

As the number of options increase, the closer they can come to resembling a continuum (the highest degree of fuzziness). And specifying points on a continuum requires the use of precise numerical values. But we all want things to be easy. Few want to deal with exact precision. So we look at reality and try to distill the essence of what we see into simple bivalent all-or-nothing categories, because "yes" and "no" are easier concepts to deal with than numbers, especially *fractions*. (Remember what part of arithmetic you hated most when you were in school?) And so we trade off reality for simplicity. We round off the fractional values of reality to the nearest "1" or "0" and pretend that *that* is reality. We pretend that fuzziness *doesn't* exist.

"The fuzzy principle has emerged from almost three thousand years of Western culture," writes Kosko, "from three thousand years of attempts to deny it, ignore it, disprove it, relabel it, and axiomatize it out of existence. But fuzziness remains despite our best efforts to get rid of it."

**Rounding Off Reality**

Find somebody whose birthday is coming up in a few days and ask them how old they are. You'll almost always get an answer like, "Right now I'm still only fifteen. But next week I'm going to be sixteen." They seem to feel that their age is some kind of "title" that becomes conferred upon them once a year on the anniversary of their birth, and that numerical "age" remains with them until their next birthday. But a person's age is not a title. Their age is a *measurement* of how many years have elapsed since the day of their birth. And a person grows older instant by instant, not year by year. You do not suddenly jump to becoming a year older on your next birthday, any more than history suddenly jumps 100 years at the turn of a century.

40    *Shades of Reality*

Rounding off is something we do almost unconsciously. For example, if we see a glass of water that is 95 percent full we refer to it as *being* full, even though the water doesn't actually quite reach the brim. Similarly, when we pour the water out of the glass we refer to the glass as then *being* empty, even though the inside walls of the glass are still wet. Except in special cases, this kind of imprecision just doesn't matter. The rounded off interpretation is sufficient for everyday use.

But if the water level in the glass is not close to one of the two extremes (full or empty), then rounding off becomes an uncomfortable process. If a glass is only halfway filled with water, should we round it *up* (and claim that the glass is *full*), or should we round it *down* (and claim that the glass is *empty*)? In this case, rounding off just doesn't work. Neither claim comes close enough to describing the reality of the matter. So we are forced into acknowledging the fuzziness — the fact that the glass is one-half full *and* one-half empty.

When we round off, we simplify to the nearest whole number (zero or one). But simplicity comes at a cost. When we simplify, we trade accuracy for convenience. Most of the time, this decrease in accuracy is negligible. However, just remember one simple rule: Everything should be made as simple as it *can* be, but no *simpler*!

Americans today even find themselves having to round off their *trash*! Instead of simply having one generic trash container for disposing refuse, it is now fashionable to have separate containers for different categories of trash (such as "paper only," "glass only," "plastic only," etc.). But what do you do when you want to throw away a glass bottle that has a paper label and a plastic cap? It doesn't completely fit into *any* of the categories, and at the same time it fits into *all* of them. And so you round it off; you say that it is *mostly* glass, so it therefore goes into the "glass only" trash container. (We will talk more about the concept of "categories" in the next chapter.)

In passing, let me just make one amusing observation about the contradictory expression, "rounding off." When we start with a

*The Smoothness Principle*     41

smooth reality (Figure 1.2) and *"round* it off," we end up creating a step function (Figure 1.1) having *square* corners!

## Rounding Off Inequalities

Two different events almost never happen at exactly the same time. Try to slap the top of a table with your left hand and right hand at exactly the same instant. You might be able to come close. But if you could measure the timing very precisely, you would probably see that you are usually off by quite a few microseconds. And yet we speak of closely occurring events as "happening at the same time." We round off the slight *in*equality to produce an equality.

Most of the time this kind of rounding off is inconsequential. But now consider the famous "stop sign dilemma:" Whenever two cars approach an intersection controlled by stop signs, the first car to arrive at the intersection has the right-of-way. However, if the two cars arrive at the "same time," then the car to the driver's right has the right-of-way.

The problem, of course, now becomes one of trying to define the boundary line that separates "equality" from "inequality." The driver on the left may have arrived at the intersection a fraction of a second ahead of the other driver. And because he got there first, he claims the right-of-way. But the driver on the right may have called their arrival times a draw, and therefore he claims the right-of-way because his car is the one on the right.

The mathematical concept of "equality" is therefore somewhat fuzzy when applied to everyday language. We will discuss the concept of fuzzy equality further in Chapter Twelve.

# Chapter Two

# Categorization

One of the hallmarks of human intelligence is the ability to form generalized concepts from specific facts. Pick up a rock. Let go of it. It falls down. Pick up a piece of wood. Let go of it. It falls down. Pick up an apple. We could go on listing things one after another. Or we could simply make the generalized statement that if you pick up *any* object and let go, it will fall down. Without the ability to generalize like this, we would have no recourse but to continue listing every specific object and explicitly stating what happens when you pick it up and then let go.

Generalization stems from the mind's ability to detect and extract patterns of similarity from otherwise unrelated entities. (A rock, a piece of wood, and an apple each have very little in common. But they all respond similarly to the operation of "pick up" followed by the operation of "let go.")

The existence of similarities provides the mind with a powerful (and often misused) tool for understanding and coping with what would otherwise be an unmanageable array of separate attributes. The process of recognizing and grouping distinct patterns of similarity is called "categorization," and the corresponding groups that result are called "categories."

## Example One:

To illustrate the concept of categorization, let's imagine that you have the collection of marbles shown in Figure 2.1, and you are told that you must divide them into two separate categories: "white" and "black." Which marbles belong to which categories?

Figure 2.1

Answer: The marbles which belong to the "white" category are: **A, B, D, H,** and **I**, while the marbles in the "black" category are: **C, E, F**, and **G**.

## Example Two:

If you thought that the previous example was trivial and foolish, then consider trying to perform exactly the same task on the collection of marbles shown in Figure 2.2:

Figure 2.2

Now the problem is *not* so trivial! Clearly, marble **A** belongs in the "white" category and marble **I** belongs in the "black" category. But what about all of the *other* marbles, the ones that are neither black nor white, but different shades of *gray*?

The usual solution to this problem is to put all of the *light* gray

## 44    *Shades of Reality*

marbles into the "white" category, and all of the *dark* gray marbles into the "black" category. But then you are still faced with the problem of deciding at which marble you should "draw the line."

Another approach to solving the problem of categorizing the marbles in Figure 2.2 might be to introduce a third *new* category called "gray." But instead of *solving* the problem, this approach only makes matters even *worse*. Now *two* "draw-the-line" points must be established, one that separates white from *almost* white, and one that separates black from *almost* black! (After all, marbles in the real world are *never* perfectly white or perfectly black.)

The most radical solution to the problem is to simply create nine separate categories, each containing a single marble! This solves the "draw-the-line" problem. But now you've merely traded nine *marbles* for nine *categories*, and so you're no better off than when you started!

### Pseudocategories

There is a good reason why you are experiencing difficulties in trying to sort the marbles in Figure 2.2 into categories: *You are trying to categorize items on the basis of an attribute whose values lie on a continuum.*

The marbles in Figure 2.1 have only two discrete color values (black and white) with no marble having an *intermediate* value. Therefore, the separation into two discrete categories is intrinsic. Furthermore, the color value of every marble in a given category is exactly the same (either black or white) as every other marble in that same category.

In the case of Figure 2.2, there *are no* intrinsic categories. If you artificially try to *force* the marbles into a small number of categories (of alleged "sameness"), you end up producing categories whose constituent members are *not* all the same. In fact it might even be possible to find two different marbles in the *same* category that have *significantly different* colors. To make matters even worse, it might even be possible to find a "white" marble and a "black" marble that are more nearly equal to *each other* than either one is to some of the other marbles in its *own category*!

This consequence is illustrated in Figure 2.3. Look at marble **E** in the "white category" and compare it to marble **F** in the "black category." There is very little difference in their colors. Their shades of gray are *almost identical* — and yet they are in two *completely separate* categories! But now compare marble **A** in the "white category" with marble **E**. Both marbles are in the *very same* category, and yet the two marbles have profoundly *different* colors!

Figure 2.3

At this point you must recall the definition of categorization: The process of grouping distinct patterns of *similarity*. If it's possible for two members of the *same* category to be significantly *different*, and if in the very same grouping it's possible for members of two *different* categories to be almost the *same,* then the attempt at categorization has obviously failed in concept.

To summarize, the process of categorization is valid only to the extent that the attribute being categorized is not represented by a continuum (or nearly a continuum).

**Attempting to partition a continuum into "categories" will generally produce groupings of questionable validity**.

I therefore refer to such attempted groupings of a partitioned continuum as forming *pseudocategories.*

However, returning once again to Figure 2.2 (or Figure 2.3),

46     *Shades of Reality*

suppose we were to simply throw away some of the "middle" gray marbles (such as **D**, **E,** and **F**) and, in their place, substitute new marbles that look more like the very light ones (such as **A**, **B**, and **C**) and/or the very dark ones (such as **G**, **H**, and **I**). Then the attempt at grouping the marbles into "black" and "white" categories *would* become more meaningful. *The less disparity that exists among the individual members of a pseudocategory, the more valid that grouping becomes* (i.e., the more the *pseudocategory* becomes a *true* category). In the extreme limit, when each of the marbles exactly resembles either marble **A** or marble **I**, then we once again have a case similar to the one shown in Figure 2.1 where the process of categorization is *completely* meaningful. (We will see in the next chapter that categories are merely examples of something known as "crisp sets," and pseudocategories are examples of something known as "fuzzy sets.")

**Example Three:**

As another example of the kinds of inconsistencies that can arise when attempting to partition a continuum into categories, consider the following advertisement that an automobile repair shop recently ran in a local newspaper:

> Special Get-Acquainted Offer!
> If your total bill is between $100 and $200 you will receive a **$10** rebate.
>
> If your total bill is between $200 and $300 you will receive a **$20** rebate.
>
> If your total bill is between $300 and $400 you will receive a **$30** rebate.
>
> etc.

The repair shop has, in effect, tried to define "categories" of

*Categorization*   47

expensiveness — those bills that total less than $200 (the *inexpensive* category), those bills that total less than $300 (the somewhat *more* expensive category), etc. But now consider two different customers, one whose total bill is $199, and the other whose total bill is $201. After their respective rebates, the first customer ends up paying $189, while the second customer's final bill is only $181. The customer whose initial bill was in the *inexpensive* "category" ends up having to pay *more* than the customer whose initial bill was more expensive!

**Lists**

Take a sheet of paper and a pencil, and make a list of all your favorite foods. You don't necessarily have to list the foods in order of preference, but the final list must be complete and accurate. In other words, you must include *every* food that you like, and *only* those foods that you like.

Initially, the task is very easy. You would probably start out by listing your *most* favorite foods. My list would start out with:

> Broiled lobster tail
> Fresh strawberry shortcake
> Macaroni and cheese
> Steamed artichokes
> Juicy cheeseburgers
> Hot buttered corn
> · · ·

Next, after you've gone through all of your very favorite foods, you would start to include those foods that you like "pretty much." In my case, they might be:

> Cookies
> Apples
> Potatoes
> · · ·

48     *Shades of Reality*

Eventually, you're going to run out of the easy items and start reaching foods like (in *my* case) lettuce, pickles, and onions (or whatever items are appropriate in *your* case). You eat these things, but is it appropriate to include them as some of your *favorite* foods? In fact, look at the very last item at the bottom of your list. Are you sure that even *that* item belongs on the list? Where do you "draw the line" between those items that *must* be included on the list, and those that must *not*? (Remember, the list must be both accurate *and* complete.)

Whenever you make a list of items, you are attempting to group the universe into two distinct categories: those items that *belong* on the list, and those items that *don't belong*. If every item on a list "belongs" on the list just as much as every other item on the list, and if every item *not* on the list "doesn't belong" on the list just as much as every other item not on the list, then the process of listing works well. For example, if I were to ask you to make a list of every state in the USA that begins with the letter **A**, you might write:

Alabama
Alaska
Arizona
Arkansas

Each of these states *belongs* on the list just as much as the other three states on the list since each one equally begins with the letter **A**. And every other state *not* on the list equally *doesn't* begin with the letter **A**. The letters of the alphabet do not form a continuum, and so the concept of an alphabetic list is valid. Furthermore, the four states on the above list are the *only* states whose names begin with the letter **A**, so the list is not only *accurate* but *complete* as well.

Similarly, if I were to ask you to list the names of all the former presidents of the United States, you would write: George Washington, John Adams, Thomas Jefferson, etc. Once again it would be possible to create a list that was both accurate and complete (since

*Categorization*   49

each of those names, and only those names, belong equally well on the list).

But not all lists can be created so "crisply." When attempting to create a list of items for which such clear-cut distinctions do not exist (such as in the case of trying to list your "favorite foods"), then the concept of listing starts to become "fuzzy." Eventually, you must deal with items that kind of *belong* on the list and which, at the same time, also kind of *don't* belong.

As another example, if someone were to try to make a list of all the "endangered species" on our planet, where would they "draw the line" between endangered and *not* endangered? And even if such a list were made, would the species at the very bottom of the list be significantly more endangered than the next species in line that *just missed* getting on the list? Would it be meaningful to say that the one species was truly endangered while the other one *wasn't* endangered at all, simply because it failed to make it onto the list? Lists are not always fair or completely accurate.

## Books

Whenever you read any non-fiction book, you will notice that the author has usually organized the book into chapters, and that each chapter may in turn be further divided into subsections. Each chapter and subsection then attempts to deal with one particular aspect of whatever subject is being presented.

But concepts are fuzzy and, as such, it is often impossible to present them in a straight linear fashion. One piece of information must overlap other similar pieces of information presented elsewhere in the book. You may notice that the author repeatedly discusses many of the same topics over and over again in different locations with each presentation coming from a slightly different perspective or in a slightly different context.

Consider the problem of trying to write a book about the history of the United States. In principle it might seem like it should be

50    *Shades of Reality*

a rather straightforward task to write such a book since history, after all, occurs linearly in time. But if a book were merely to present history as a series of chronological events, then it would not be able to discuss *parallel* developments taking place in other parts of the country. Nor would it be able to follow a single topic (such as the life of Abraham Lincoln) and continue to focus on that particular aspect of American history for any length of time.

And just as in the case of lists, the author must also decide which topics he considers to be important enough to be *included* in the book, and which ones will "just miss" making it in. In most cases, it would simply be impossible (or impractical) to include every single topic or event. For example, a "complete" book of American history would have to include all biographies (even yours and mine) since we too are a part of ongoing history.

And even for those topics that do get included, the author must decide to what extent they will be discussed before moving on to a new topic.

Suppose it were possible (at least in principle) to discuss every single aspect of a topic and to present it from all conceivable points of view. But even if such an approach were possible, such an extreme analysis of a subject could become rather boring for the reader. It is usually better to simply say what needs to be said without wasting time covering redundant and irrelevant material just for the sake of completeness. Of course this will require that some material will, of necessity, be presented only partially or superficially. But that is the price one must pay for brevity. It is far better to cover the most relevant topics more thoroughly so that the reader can grasp the essential ideas. It is therefore OK to completely eliminate some aspects of any given topic, and to consider the subject matter appropriately covered by those aspects that *are* explained.

## Equification

As was already pointed out, the process of categorization is

*Categorization* 51

valid only to the extent that the attribute being categorized is not represented by a continuum. But despite the warning of trying to attach a meaningful interpretation to the elements of a partitioned continuum, society still goes ahead and does it anyway. Grocery stores, for example, like to sort their fruits and vegetables into different *size* categories — "small" tomatoes vs. "large" tomatoes, "jumbo" artichokes vs. "medium" artichokes, and so on — as if nature *really* grew them in only one size or the other! And in many cases, the method of partitioning is so extreme that the entire size continuum is actually reduced to only a *single* "category"! (In this case the item is simply sold "by the piece," regardless of any size differences between the items.)

But regardless of the number of partitions used, there seems to be one common "mind-set" that almost always arises about the individual items in each pseudocategory. Borrowing from a certain well-known document written by Thomas Jefferson ("We hold these truths to be self-evident, that all vegetables are created equal . . ."), I define:

### *Equification*

**The pretense that all of the individual items
in a given pseudocategory are exactly equal.**

For example equification declares that every "large" tomato is *exactly* the same as every other "large" tomato. If the price of one "large" tomato is 79 cents, then the price of any other "large" tomato is also 79 cents, even if one of the tomatoes is somewhat smaller than the other.

## All-or-Nothingism

There is one particular form of equification that is so prevalent in our society that I have given it a name of its own. It occurs when a continuum is partitioned into exactly two pseudocategories, and when all of the members of one of the pseudocategories are equified

## 52    *Shades of Reality*

to some *maximum* value, while all of the members of the other pseudocategory are equified to a value of *zero*. I call this form of equification — **All-or-Nothingism.**

Examples of All-or-Nothingism are abundant in everyday life. To discuss them all thoroughly would require a separate book. But the following illustrate a few representative examples:

- If you are an American citizen *over* the age of 18, you get to vote. (vote = 1). If you are an American citizen *under* the age of 18, you get *no* vote. (vote = 0).

- In California if you park your car near a curb that is painted red, you are subject to receiving a parking ticket if any part of your car overlaps the red part of the curb. If you do not overlap this "red zone," you will *not* receive a parking ticket.

- If you arrive at a concert (or sporting event, etc.) late and miss part of the show, you are still charged the *full price* of admission. But if you arrive after some prescribed time (or after the ticket-taker has gone home), you get in *free of charge*.

- If you are over the age of 21, you *can* legally drink alcoholic beverages. If you are less than 21 years of age, you *cannot* legally drink any amount of alcohol. (A person who is 20 years old and a newborn baby both are *exactly* identical insofar as their legal right to drink alcoholic beverages!)

- If a student's test score exceeds a specified value, he *passes* the test. Otherwise, he/she completely *fails* the test.

- If a packaged food item has a *future* expiration date stamped on the package, the food in the package is still "fresh." Otherwise, if the expiration date is in the *past*, the food is "old" and should be thrown out. (I've seen some

*Categorization*     53

food packages, like breakfast cereals, that have expiration dates well over a *year* into the future. And yet those dates of expiration are specified right down to the very *day*! Is it really possible that after sitting on the shelf for more than a year, food can just suddenly change from being totally *fresh* to totally *bad* overnight?)

- Near propane filling stations, no open flames are allowed at a distance of 25 feet or less. At a distance of more than 25 feet, it's perfectly OK. (For some unknown reason we seem to feel that "safe" suddenly turns into "not safe" at some well-defined number of feet and inches!)

- Some drugs (such as heroine, cocaine, etc.) are to be *completely avoided*, while other drugs (like alcohol, tobacco, etc.) are *just fine* (and are even socially acceptable)!

- Abortions performed before ___ weeks of pregnancy (you fill in the blank) are *perfectly acceptable*. After that time, it is *completely wrong* to have an abortion ("pro-choice" view).

- "Abortions" performed before conception are *perfectly acceptable*. After that time, it is *completely wrong* to have an abortion ("pro-life" view).

- A creature is either a human being or else it isn't. If it *is* human, then it is "endowed by its Creator with certain unalienable Rights." If it is *not* human, then it *isn't* so endowed.

- If you are an American citizen age 35 or older, you are equally qualified to run for the office of President. If you are less than 35 years of age, you are equally *non*-qualified, just like everyone else who is less than 35 years of age.

54    *Shades of Reality*

- In an election, or in any competitive event (sports, games, etc.), the person (or team) that comes out on top is *the winner*. Everyone else is just a "loser," regardless of how close the results were.

- In football, if one of the players commits a foul (such as "unnecessary roughness"), the game official declares a penalty and yardage is marked off. But if the player uses just enough *less* roughness, no penalty is called and *no yardage* gets marked off.

- If you've lived your life well enough, you'll go to heaven when you die. Otherwise, you'll go to hell (and be with everyone else who was absolutely and totally evil, just like you!).

As silly and unrealistic as most of these equifications are, almost nobody seems to question them! They represent a mind-set so firmly rooted in our Aristotelian way of thinking that most of Western society actually seems to accept them as being perfectly logical. (After all, you 'gotta' draw the line *somewhere*, right?)

We will return to discussions of "drawing the line" and other such all-or-nothing concepts many times throughout the remainder of this book.

# Chapter Three

# Fuzzy Logic

The patterns in thinking of Western civilization have their roots in ancient Greece. More than two thousand years ago Aristotle formulated the laws of logic that, even today, profoundly affect the ways in which we view and discuss reality.

According to Aristotle's way of thinking, logic was a binary operation: something was either **A**, or else it was **not-A**. Grass was either green, or else it was not green. It certainly couldn't be both green *and* not-green simultaneously. It had to be one or the other. Therefore, any statement (such as, "grass is green") could be assigned a numerical truth value: If the statement was true, it's truth value was 1 (or 100 percent); if the statement was false, it's truth value was 0 (or 0 percent).

As we have already seen, reality has a smoothness to it. For example, "day" continuously turns into "not-day" without crossing any well-defined boundary line. Reality, therefore, does not always seem to conform very well to Aristotelian black and white logic, a fact that (ironically) was largely ignored by science, the very discipline that *supposedly* studies reality! Scientists and mathematicians still continued to view the world as a black and white place that had

56    *Shades of Reality*

well-defined yes or no answers to all questions. Every molecule in the universe was either a part of your body, or else it wasn't. Every mathematical statement was either a true statement, or else it was a false statement. Everything was either *all*, or else it was *nothing*.

**Sets**

In the late 19th century Georg Cantor, a German mathematician, developed a branch of mathematics known as *set theory*. Cantor defined sets as collections of definite, distinguishable objects of our intuition or intellect. For example, the set of single-digit perfect squares would be: 0, 1, 4, and 9.

For the purposes of visualization, sets are sometimes depicted as circles (Venn diagrams), which divide the "universe" into two parts. The part *inside* a particular circle represents those objects that *belong* to that particular set, and the part *outside* the circle represents those objects that *do not* belong to the set. (Those objects that belong to the set are usually called *elements* of the set, and the region outside the set is referred to as the *complement* of the set.) For example the point **a** in Figure 3.1 is a member of the set **S** (the horizontally shaded region), while the point **b** is not a member of **S**. Instead, point **b** is a member of the set **Not S** (the vertically shaded region), which is the *complement* of the set **S**.

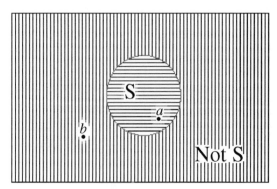

Figure 3.1

*Fuzzy Logic*     57

For any particular set (such as **S**), every object in the universe (or "universal set" defined in Figure 3.1 as the complete rectangle) is either a member of that set, or else it is not a member (i.e., it is either a member of the set **S**, or else it is a member of the set **Not S**). There can be no objects that are only partly in the set and partly out. Membership in a set is *all*, or *nothing*.

When the universal set consists of an innumerable collection of items, it is also customary to represent a particular set as a sequence of ones and zeros, which specifically indicate those items of the universal set that *are* contained in the set and those that are *not*. To create such a sequence of ones and zeros, simply write down all of the individual items of the universal set in some prescribed order. Then underneath each item write down a one (if that item is a part of the set) or a zero (if that item is not a part of the set). For example if our universal set consists of the single-digit integers, then to represent our previous set of perfect squares (0, 1, 4, and 9) we would proceed as follows:

$$0 \; 1 \; 2 \; 3 \; 4 \; 5 \; 6 \; 7 \; 8 \; 9$$
$$1 \; 1 \; 0 \; 0 \; 1 \; 0 \; 0 \; 0 \; 0 \; 1$$

Therefore the set of single-digit perfect squares would be represented by the sequence: (1, 1, 0, 0, 1, 0, 0, 0, 0, 1). Similarly, the set of single-digit odd integers would be represented by the sequence: (0, 1, 0, 1, 0, 1, 0, 1, 0, 1).

As successful as Cantor's set theory became, it still had difficulties handling a certain kind of scenario known as a *sorites* paradox: Take a heap of sand. Remove one grain of sand from the heap. Is it still a heap? Remove another grain, and another. Eventually, you'll end up with only one grain of sand left. At which point did the heap become *not* a heap? Or, in terms of set theory, which of the intermediate stages belong to the set called "heaps," and which ones don't? Of course the traditional way such a problem is resolved is to simply "draw the line" at some arbitrary point — declare some minimum threshold value as the fewest number of grains of sand that

## 58    *Shades of Reality*

you will acknowledge as being a heap. Once the size of the pile diminishes past that point, it is no longer a heap. But this "draw the line" philosophy, while presenting a pragmatic "solution" to the problem, merely sidesteps the real issue — a fundamental inadequacy in the concept of all-or-nothing sets.

### Vagueness

Things in the real world tend to have vague boundary lines. For example there is no precise point in time at when day becomes night, as we have already discussed in Chapter One in conjunction with the Smoothness Principle.

It is important to distinguish vagueness from uncertainty. There are many things in the universe that are uncertain, like "Is it going to rain one month from today?" or "Did life ever exist on the planet Mars?" or "What's the real story behind the JFK assassination?" These kinds of questions have answers, which may be uncertain today, but given more information may ultimately be resolved. (If we simply wait one more month, we will know for certain whether or not it is going to rain.)

Vagueness, on the other hand, is an intrinsic property that *doesn't* go away when more information is supplied. Even if we had all the information in the universe at our disposal, and even if we could ask God for the answers, we *still* couldn't resolve vagueness.

The American philosopher Charles Pierce (1839-1914) was one of the first persons to formally investigate vagueness. He maintained that all that exists is continuous, and such continua govern knowledge. For example, both size and time exist as continua. So even though an acorn will eventually become an oak tree, it is impossible to determine a point in time when the transition occurs. This kind of vagueness is not simply the result of faulty *thinking* on our part. The uncertainty is inherent in *reality*. "Vagueness," he said, "is no more to be done away with in the real world of logic than friction in mechanics."

*Fuzzy Logic*     59

In 1923 Bertrand Russell published a paper in which he argued that vagueness was merely a feature of human language, rather than an aspect of reality. Furthermore, he contended, vagueness was clearly a matter of degree.

In 1937 quantum philosopher Max Black published a paper titled "Vagueness: An Exercise in Logical Analysis." In his paper he stated that vagueness arises from continua, and that continua imply degrees. Furthermore, a continuum did not have to actually be continuous. Even discrete entities, which form *nearly* a continuum will still result in vagueness (as we saw in our discussion of pseudo-categories in the previous chapter).

The example Black gave was to imagine a row of chairs stretching toward the horizon. The front-most chair is a Chippendale, and behind it is a near-Chippendale, which is almost indistinguishable from the one in front of it. Succeeding chairs become even less and less chair-like until, at the end of the row, there is a block of raw wood. So, even in this case, the concept of "chair" does not have a distinct separation from the concept of "not-chair." However, when dealing with such a "continuum of discretes," one can stick a number on each item in the row, and that number will indicate the degree to which that item can be regarded as being a "chair."

As a more modern example of the same idea, consider the process of "morphing" an image on a computer. The user supplies digitized photographs of two entirely different objects (such as a person's face and a dog's face). The computer then generates a sequence of in-between images that starts with one of the initial two images, and eventually ends with the second image. However, the difference between any two consecutive images is negligible, and so it is impossible to determine a specific frame number at which the image changes from that of a person to that of a dog.

The ideas that Max Black expressed in 1937 are virtually identical to the concepts that today are known as "fuzzy logic." But because he published in a journal that almost no one had heard of, and

## 60    *Shades of Reality*

because of the strong counteropinions that prevailed at the time, his ideas fell into obscurity, and he never again pursued the matter.

### Fuzzy Sets

In 1920 a Polish logician and philosopher by the name of Jan Lucasiewicz published a paper describing a new system of logic. Just as in Aristotle's logic, zero represented false, and one represented true. But Lucasiewicz introduced a *new* value, 1/2, which stood for *possible* (or *indeterminate*). A statement could therefore have any one of these *three* truth values. This line of thinking immediately opened the door for the next obvious step — why use only *one* intermediate point? And so, ultimately, he assigned a continuum of points between true (1) and false (0), with each fractional value representing a *degree* of truth. (We will discuss more about truth in the next chapter.)

In 1965 Professor Lotfi Zadeh of the University of California published a paper called "Fuzzy Sets," in which he applied Lucasiewicz's multi-valued logic to the concepts of sets. As you recall, in a traditional set, membership is an all-or-nothing concept. Consequently the statement, "point **a** (in Figure 3.1) is a member of set **S**," is a statement whose truth value is equal to one. And the statement, "point **b** is a member of set **S**," is a statement whose truth value is equal to zero.

But if one allows multi-valued logic to be applied to statements about membership, then it allows for the existence of a new kind of set — one in which statements about membership can have truth values anywhere in the range from zero to one. In other words, the set can contain members that only *partly* belong to the set, and at the same time, also partly *don't* belong to it. And the degree to which a member belongs to the set is indicated by its *membership value*, a number that can range anywhere from zero (for total nonmembership) to one (for total membership). While it is customary to express membership values in the range 0 to 1.0, it is also permissible to express them as *percentages*. In this case the values will, of course, range from 0 percent to 100 percent.

Zadeh called his new sets "fuzzy sets" to distinguish them from the "crisp" sets of Cantor. (If Max Black had received the recognition he deserved for making essentially the same observations back in 1937, such sets would have been known today as "vague sets.") It is perhaps somewhat unfortunate that Zadeh chose the name, "fuzzy," to describe his sets. The concept of a fuzzy set is already too strange for the average American to understand. And the use of such a silly sounding name just opens up the whole idea to ridicule by those who understand the concept the least. Also the term "fuzzy" erroneously conjures up an image of tiny hair-like substances (like cotton fuzz or peach fuzz), which if magnified sufficiently should ultimately resolve into well-defined structures. Perhaps a better name might have been something like *blurred* sets, or *smooth* sets. But for better or for worse, the name *fuzzy* has stuck.

A fuzzy set is not a new *separate* kind of set; fuzzy sets *include* crisp sets. A crisp set is merely a fuzzy set whose elements all have membership values of only zero or one. The relationship between a fuzzy set and its complement is illustrated in Figure 3.2.

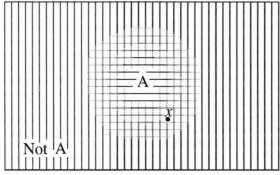

Figure 3.2

In this illustration the horizontally shaded circular region represents a fuzzy set **A**, and the vertically shaded region represents

## 62    *Shades of Reality*

**not A**, the complement set. Any point, such as x, exists in a region that is both horizontally shaded to some degree and vertically shaded to some degree. The darker the horizontal shading, the greater the membership value in the set **A**. The darker the vertical shading, the greater the membership value in the *complement* of the set (i.e., the more the point is "in **not A**," or equivalently "not in **A**"). Furthermore, the sum total of an element's membership value in a fuzzy set plus its membership value in the complement of the set add up to one (or 100 percent), just as they do in the case of crisp sets.

### Example: Tall Men

The traditional example of a fuzzy set is the set of tall men. Suppose we have five men named Al, Bill, Charlie, Dave, and Ed. Al's height is 5'7", Bill is 5'9", Charlie is 5'11", Dave is 6'1", and Ed is 6'3". Using *conventional* thinking we might ask the question, "which of these men are *tall* (or equivalently, which men are members of the set called "tall men")? The usual procedure for answering this question is to assign an arbitrary cutoff point at some height and then define "tall" as being any height greater than that value. Therefore, if we were to arbitrarily draw a mental boundary line at 5'10", we would say that Charlie, Dave, and Ed are tall men (i.e., they are members of the set called "tall men"), while Al and Bill are not.

In contrast, *fuzzy* thinking embodies the smoothness principle — everything (including "tallness") happens smoothly. So instead of trying to establish an unrealistic cutoff point between tall and not tall, fuzzy logic asks the question, "to what *degree* are each of the men tall (i.e., to what degree are they members of the "tall men" set)? For example the statement, "Ed is a tall man," might have a truth value of 0.9, while the corresponding statement about Al might have a truth value of only about 0.2. Therefore, Ed would have a 90 percent membership value in the "tall men" set, while Al's membership value in the set would be only 20 percent.

## Fuzzy Logic   63

The fuzzy approach to sets clearly supplies more information about membership than does the conventional crisp approach. Instead of supplying only simple "yes" or "no" answers, fuzzy sets specify *numerical* information indicating the *degree* of membership. Therefore, the *fuzzy* approach is, ironically, the more *precise* approach!

### Example: Pitching Pennies

Let's look at one more example that will show how fuzzy sets and crisp sets relate to each other as well as to our everyday use of language. Figure 3.3 shows the game of "Pitching Pennies."

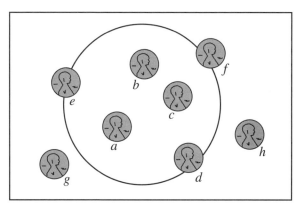

Figure 3.3

The object of the game is to toss a penny so that it ends up inside the circle. If I were to ask the question, "of the eight coins shown in Figure 3.3, which ones lie completely inside the circle"? the answer would be the crisp set consisting of the coins, **a**, **b**, and **c**. This set could also be expressed as a binary sequence by associating each element of the universal set (**a** through **h**) with either a zero or a one:

**a b c d e f g h**
**1 1 1 0 0 0 0 0**

64     *Shades of Reality*

Therefore, the set coins that lie completely inside the circle would be represented by the sequence: (1,1,1,0,0,0,0,0).

However, if I omit the word "completely," the question itself becomes vague. Should the coins, **d**, **e**, and **f**, be considered as lying "inside" the circle or "outside" the circle? To some degree they are *both*. Therefore, the answer to the vague question would be the *fuzzy set* consisting of the coins, **a**, **b**, **c**, **d**, **e**, and **f**. The three coins, **a**, **b**, and **c**, would each have a membership value of 100 percent, while the remaining three coins, **d**, **e**, and **f**, would have membership values of approximately 75 percent, 50 percent, and 25 percent, respectively. (Even coins **g** and **h** could be considered as lying "inside" the circle — but to a zero degree.) I could also rephrase the question slightly and ask, "to what degree is each coin inside the circle? And once again the same corresponding percentages would answer this new question.

Just as in the case of crisp sets, a fuzzy set can also be represented by a sequence of "binary-type" numbers. But since each member of the fuzzy set can have a membership value anywhere in the range from zero to one, the sequence of numbers representing the fuzzy set will not be limited to consisting of combinations of only zeros and ones. The sequence will generally have fractional values as well. Therefore, the fuzzy set of coins lying inside the circle would be represented by the sequence:

$$(1, \ 1, \ 1, \ 3/4, \ 1/2, \ 1/4, \ 0, \ 0)$$

Finally, suppose I were to ask a question about one of the border-touching coins: "Is coin **f** inside of the circle"? We will discuss this kind of question (and its answer) in the next chapter.

### White & Black Marbles

Let's now return to our discussion of partitioned continua that we began in the previous chapter. In the light of our ongoing discussion, it should be obvious that pseudocategories are nothing more

*Fuzzy Logic*     65

than fuzzy sets. If one partitions a continuum into pseudocategories, then the closer an item is to the "boundary line" of that partitioning, the more it becomes a member of *both* sets.

For example consider the two fuzzy sets, "White marbles" and "Black marbles," which were depicted in Figure 2.3 in Chapter Two. We now realize that instead of simply asking which marbles "belong" to a given set, we must ask what each marble's *membership value* is in that particular set. The set of "White marbles" shown in Figure 2.3 might be represented by the sequence:

$$(1, \ 7/8, \ 3/4, \ 5/8, \ 1/2, \ 3/8, \ 1/4, \ 1/8, \ 0)$$

where marble **A** has a membership value of 1, marble **B** has a membership value of 7/8, etc.

Since in this example, the sets "White marbles" and "Black marbles" are complementary sets (i.e., "Black marbles" is "Not-White marbles"), then each marble's membership value on the "Black marbles" set must be equal to one minus its membership value in the "White marbles" set. Therefore, the set of "Black marbles" would be represented by the sequence:

$$(0, \ 1/8, \ 1/4, \ 3/8, \ 1/2, \ 5/8, \ 3/4, \ 7/8, \ 1)$$

Notice that the fifth marble in this example has a membership value of 1/2 in *both* sets. It is as much "white" as it is "black." And equivalently, it is as much "not white" as it is "not black." It is at this point that a "white" marble becomes indistinguishable from a "black" marble. It is here that the concept, **A = Not-A**, holds exactly.

**Getting Dark**

Our preceding three examples (Tall Men, Pitching Pennies, and White and Black Marbles) were all instances of fuzzy sets whose members consisted of *discrete* entities (men, coins, and marbles). Because there was only a finite number of them, the membership values in these sets could be simply enumerated. But

## 66    Shades of Reality

how would we indicate the membership values for fuzzy sets that contain an *infinite* number of members?

As an example of a fuzzy set whose members form a *continuum*, let's return to our discussion from Chapter One about when the sky gets dark. It should be obvious by now that the collection of clock times that represent periods of darkness constitute a fuzzy set. Each point in time is therefore a member of the "Dark" set to some degree, and also *not* a member to some degree. As the sun sets and the sky continues to get darker and darker, each successive point in time gradually becomes more and more of a member of the fuzzy set called "Dark."

One way to approximate this fuzzy set might be to indicate membership values for only a few selected points equally spaced in time. For example if we were to start at sunset and specify the level of darkness at ten-minute intervals, we might produce something like the following sequence for the "Dark" set:

$$(0.05,\ 0.15,\ 0.40,\ 0.65,\ 0.85,\ 0.95)$$

Sunset would have only about 0.05 membership value in the "Dark" set, ten minutes past sunset would have a membership value of about 0.15, etc.

If we wanted to, we could plot these values on a graph and obtain a set of dots showing a *visual* representation of the "Dark" set:

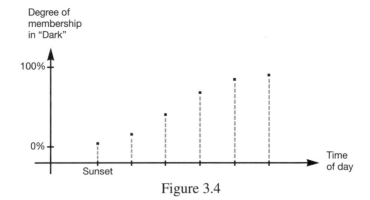

Figure 3.4

## Fuzzy Logic   67

If we were to do the same construction using five-minute intervals instead of ten-minute intervals, we would produce an even better visual representation of the "Dark" set. (We would fill in some of the intermediate points.) And finally, if we were to use infinitesimally small intervals of time, we would end up with a *smooth curve* representing the "Dark" set:

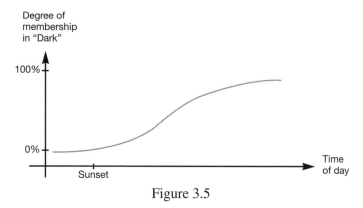

Figure 3.5

From such a curve, we can simply "read off" the membership value at any point by measuring the height of the curve at that point.

We will be using many such curves to denote fuzzy sets, particularly in Part Two of this book.

# Chapter Four

# Truth and Knowledge

When we make a statement, we assert a description of some aspect of reality. The extent to which the statement conforms to fact is a measure of the *truth* of the statement.

Philosophers distinguish *logical* truth from *descriptive* truth. Statements that indicate logical or mathematical relationships (such as: $3 + 2 = 5$) are referred to as logical truths, while statements that specify facts about physical reality (such as: "The Earth is round") are referred to as descriptive truths.

The Polish logician, Alfred Tarski, expressed the relationship between descriptive statements and their truth. His *statement formula of truth* says:

> "STATEMENT" is true if and only if STATEMENT.

The left-most term, "STATEMENT" (in quotes), indicates an assertion. The right-most term, STATEMENT, describes a fact. (In other words, "STATEMENT" are the actual *words* we use to express the fact.) For example, the statement "The sky is blue" is true if and only if the sky is blue. And *"Der Himmel ist blau"* is true if and only if the sky is blue.

*Truth and Knowledge*     69

Fuzzy logic views truth as accuracy, and accuracy is obviously a matter of degree. Statements of logical truths are always either 100 percent accurate or 0 percent accurate. But statements about physical reality have accuracy values that lie in between these extremes.

*Words represent fuzzy sets.* For example a term like "blue" does not have one and only one precise meaning. The word "blue" includes a continuum of possible colors: light blue, baby blue, azure blue, powder blue, etc., each having a slightly different membership value in the set called "blue." And so a statement like "The sky is blue" is accurate only to the extent that the sky's actual color is a member of the "blue" set. (We will return to this concept in Chapter Six.)

## Truth is a Matter of Degree

The more accurately a statement describes reality, the more *truthful* the statement is. And to whatever extent the statement inaccurately describes reality, the more *false* the statement is. *All statements are therefore both true to some degree, and false to some degree.* Even statements of logical truth (such as "2 + 2 = 4") are both true to *some* degree and false to *some* degree — their degree of truth is 100 percent, and their degree of falseness is 0 percent. (Of course an incorrect statement, such as "2 + 2 = *3*," is 0 percent true and 100 percent *false*.)

Other statements whose degree of truth can be 100 percent are statements of *establishment* (or *definition*). For example the statement, "The city of Madison is the capitol of Wisconsin," is a statement whose degree of truth is 100 percent, simply because Madison was *established* (or *defined*) as being the capitol of Wisconsin. These kinds of statements reflecting such "man-made" truths are therefore tautologically true. However, as we pointed out in Chapter Zero, man-made "truths" are (in general) only as *true* as they are *consistent*.

70    *Shades of Reality*

In summary, statements of truth can be classified into three general types:

- **Logical** (or Mathematical) Truths (e.g., "8 − 3 = 5")

- **Established** (or Defined) Truths (e.g., "George Washington was the first president of the United States.")

- **Descriptive** Truths about Physical Reality (e.g., "Today is a cloudy day.")

## Is It Dark Yet?

Let us return now to the discussion we started in Chapter One about what point in time the sky gets dark. The terms "day" and "night" represent fuzzy sets. Therefore, any point in time has some degree of membership in both sets. And since the "night" set is the complement of the "day" set, the sum of the membership values in the two sets for any point must be 100 percent.

If at some point in time, someone were to make the statement: "The sky is dark." That statement would have a degree of truth somewhere between 0 percent and 100 percent, depending on the time's membership value in the "night" set. Similarly, the statement would have a degree of falseness (equal to 100 percent minus the degree of truth). For example if the statement were to be 83 percent true, then it would also be 17 percent false. So at that particular point in time, the question, "Is it dark yet"? *would* have an answer. The answer would be: 83 percent *yes*, and 17 percent *no*!

Also along these same lines, in the previous chapter I asked the question: "Is coin $f$ (in Figure 3.3) inside of the circle"? By exactly the same reasoning, the answer to that question would be 25 percent *yes*, and 75 percent *no*.

## Degrees Of "Yes" And "No"

It is very important that you fully understand this concept of

*Truth and Knowledge* 71

partially "yes" and partially "no" (or "yes" to some degree, and "no" to some degree) as being a valid answer to a question. Such an answer does *not* mean that I can't make up my mind about which choice is the correct answer. Nor does it mean that I'm being wishy-washy by trying to avoid answering the question. An answer of "yes" to some degree and "no" to some degree *is* the answer to the question.

Most people find it difficult to comprehend this apparent contradiction. They've been brought up to think that all questions should always have answers that can ultimately simplify to a "bottom line" result of either completely "yes," or else completely "no." They feel that it's got to end up being one way or the other. But the answer of "yes" to some specified degree and "no" to some specified degree *is* the "bottom line" result.

Of course you can always *pretend* that it's OK to somehow round off this "bottom line" result to the nearest "yes" or "no." But if you don't want to accept the *correct* answer as it stands, then you can *pretend* anything you like! (It's always possible to find "easy" answers to *any* question, if you don't mind having *wrong* answers!)

Consider an airplane pilot who wanted to fly from Miami, Florida, to Seattle, Washington. He looked on a map and asked himself the question: "Is Seattle north of Miami, or is Seattle west of Miami"? The correct answer, of course, is that Seattle is both north to some degree, and west to some degree. But our pilot didn't like having to deal with reality and its confusing fractions and percentages. So he decided to round off the correct answer to the nearest "north" or "west," and then he chose *that* direction in which to fly. (He's still looking for Seattle, but at least he has an easier course to follow!)

**How To Ask Questions**

Truth is a matter of *degree*, and this degree must always be acknowledged *somewhere*. Therefore, any question involving a truth must either:

72    *Shades of Reality*

a) expect an answer which contains some degree of "yes" and some degree of "no," or else,

b) be asked in such a way that the question *itself* contains an acknowledgment of degree.

The two options are equivalent and the choice of which one to use is entirely up to you. Therefore, if you feel uneasy with fuzzy answers (ones that are "partially yes" and "partially no"), then simply refrain from asking questions that *require* such answers. Instead, rephrase your questions in such a way that they explicitly request answers involving indications of *degree*. In other words, instead of expressing questions in the form:

Is "STATEMENT" true?

simply ask the equivalent question:

To what *degree* is "STATEMENT" true?

Since the question *itself* then acknowledges the concept of degree, the answer can now be crisp rather than fuzzy. For example instead of asking a question like, "Is it dark"? simply rephrase the question so that it now becomes: "To what *degree* is it dark"? or more simply: "*How* dark is it"? This will allow for a more traditional-sounding answer.

## Disputes and Disagreements

We all live in the same physical world, and we are all members of the same species (*Homo sapiens*). And yet, we all have slightly different philosophies. Some of us are Liberals, and some of us are Conservatives. Some of us are pro-life, and some of us are pro-choice. Some of us are Republicans, and some of us are Democrats. Some of us are in favor of having strict gun control laws, and some of us oppose the idea.

*Truth and Knowledge*     73

And we even have our own private disputes. The other driver claims that *you* ran into *him*, and you claim that *he* failed to yield to *you*. *You* say that your next-door neighbor is making too much noise, and *he* claims that he isn't. The *cop* claims that you were driving at night without your headlights on, and *you* claim that it was not yet dark.

But if we're all involved in the very same physical reality, then how come there are such disagreements? If there is only one true reality, then shouldn't one side or the other ultimately end up being proven to be the *correct* side?

There's an old adage which says: "There are two sides to every argument." Of course the traditional interpretation of this saying is simply: don't try to determine who's right and who's wrong until both sides have had a chance to present their cases. However, since truth is a matter of degree, a more realistic interpretation of the adage presents itself — an interpretation that does not require the eventual choosing of a correct side: *Both* sides of any argument are usually right — to some degree — and, of course, both sides are usually wrong, also to some degree.

In almost every argument, both sides feel that their claims are legitimate — and they usually are. But each side sees only its own "rightness" and only the other side's "wrongness." Therefore, it's easy for each side to claim that its own view is *totally* right while that of the opposition is totally *wrong*. Moreover, each side generally seems to think that by merely being able to successfully defend his own position, that he will have therefore somehow "disproved" the *opposing* view. And so each side usually tries to "win" the argument by focusing exclusively on his or her *own* merits, while totally ignoring the valid counterarguments of the *other* side.

Most arguments can be resolved fairly and accurately, not by looking for an absolute "winner," but by acknowledging the degrees of rightness and wrongness of *both* sides of the argument. (But trying to get both factions to *accept* this fair and accurate resolution may pose a problem!)

74    *Shades of Reality*

**Telling the Truth**

In a court of law, witnesses are instructed to "tell the truth, the whole truth, and nothing but the truth." This means that they are not allowed to *omit* portions of the truth (they must tell the *whole* truth), nor are they allowed to *add* false testimony to otherwise true statements (they must tell *nothing but* the truth). In other words, their testimony must be both accurate and complete.

But as we have already seen, truth is a matter of degree. Therefore, every statement (except for logically true statements and statements of definition) contains at least some small degree of falseness. And so making *any* statement (even supposedly "true" ones) would not comply with the directive to tell "nothing *but* the truth!" And yet *not* to make any statement would violate the directive to tell "the *whole* truth"! (The dilemma is similar to the one in Chapter Two where you were told to make an accurate and complete list of all your favorite foods.) And so it is generally impossible to comply with a court's request for such black and white testimony.

**Knowledge**

Truths exist independently from us. If all of mankind were to disappear from the universe, the fact that $2 + 2 = 4$ would still be true. But we *do* exist, and we are aware. When we become aware of a truth, we say that we *know* that truth. Knowledge is therefore awareness of a truth.

Let's play a little game. I'm thinking of a number. Can you tell me what the number is? Of course not. I could be thinking of *any* number. It could be five. Or it could be -7.38. I might even be thinking of one million times the square root of *pi*.

But now suppose I were to tell you that the number that I'm thinking of is an integer. Now can you tell me which number I'm thinking of? No, but you can eliminate a lot of possibilities. For

*Truth and Knowledge*        75

example you now know that I'm not thinking of a fraction, and I'm not thinking of an irrational number or a number with a decimal point somewhere between two of its digits.

Next, suppose I tell you that the number is less than 100.

Suppose I tell you that it's greater than 20 but less than 30.

Suppose I tell you the number is more than 22 but less than 27.

Suppose I tell you the number is more than 24.9 but less than 25.1.

"Aha"! you say. "The number you're thinking of is 25."

"Correct!" I reply.

But now let me ask you one more question: *When* did you *know* that the number was 25? You would probably say that you *knew* it after I gave the last clue, because 25 is the only integer between 24.9 and 25.1. And prior to hearing that clue you had no idea what number I was thinking of.

We tend to use expressions like "I had no idea" in a rather cavalier way. While it may be true that you *initially* "had no idea" what the number was, you at least knew that I was thinking of a *number*. I was not thinking of a letter of the alphabet, nor was I thinking of a color in the rainbow, nor was I thinking of a city in the United States, etc. (If I had merely said that I was thinking of *something*, then you might truly have "had no idea" what I was thinking of.) As each new clue came, you were able to add more and more items to the list of things that I was *not* thinking of. In other words, your knowledge about what I *was* thinking of continued to increase. By the time that I was ready to give you the very last clue, you already had a pretty good approximation of the number, even though you may not have known it completely and precisely.

Still, you might want to insist on adopting the all-or-nothing stance that either you know the number completely, or else you don't know it at all. (Old habits and old ways of thinking die hard!) In response to your objection I'll ask you another question: "Do you know the value of *pi*"? The numerical value of *pi* has the

## 76  *Shades of Reality*

approximate value, 3.1416. But *pi* is an irrational number with an infinite number of digits. Nobody could ever know what every single one of those digits is. And so, by your reasoning, nobody has the slightest idea of what the value of *pi* is!

If you're still not convinced that knowledge is a matter of degree, then let's invoke a "smoothness principle" type of approach. At what *precise point in time* did you know the correct answer to our number guessing game? After you had read *halfway* though the final clue? After you had read *three-quarters* of the way through the final clue? After you reached the *period* at the end of the clue's sentence?

Your brain didn't *instantaneously* create the correct answer of 25. It took at least several milliseconds to even *comprehend* the final clue, and then at least several more milliseconds to calculate the answer. You didn't just suddenly "see the light" in zero time. Instead, the light took a small but finite amount of time to gradually come on. Even this analysis shows that, at any instant in time, knowledge is present in degrees.

When you were in school and took a class in a certain subject, at what point in time did you completely "know" the course material? When you attended the first day of the class? Halfway through the semester? After the very last lecture? After you completed the final exam? In fact, did you *ever* completely "know" the course material?

And speaking of the final exam, if you missed one or more questions on that exam, was that an indication that you didn't know *any* of the course material? Instead of receiving a passing grade, should you have failed the course merely because you didn't remember or understand every single thing that was taught to you?

Knowledge is *not* something that you either have or don't have. Knowledge is not an absolute. *All knowledge is a matter of degree.*

### Forgetting

Likewise, *forgetting* is also a matter of degree. While you are reading a book or attending a lecture, the material is still fresh in

*Truth and Knowledge* 77

your mind. But as time passes, you start forgetting it little by little. After a while certain specific facts may still remain in your memory, but others start to blur out. For example, you no doubt remember that George Washington was the first president of the United States. And you probably even recall that his birthday is sometime in February. But unless you make it your business to memorize such things, you might not remember exactly *which* day it is.

Forgetting, therefore, represents a *diminishing level of knowledge with time*. And unless you have a brain disorder (such as amnesia) you don't generally forget everything all at once. Nor do you generally forget things in an all-or-nothing manner. Even when you think that you've totally forgotten a piece of information, hearing that information again will usually "ring a bell" because some degree of that knowledge still remains in your mind. (That is why some schools offer "refresher courses" in certain subjects.)

There are definite procedures that you can use to improve your ability to remember things, and there are a number of institutions that offer "memory classes." The fundamental idea taught in these classes is the relatively simple trick of associating specific pieces of information with visual images. In Rex Dante's memory classes he used a process that he called the "TAVE" method (an acronym for: Touch, Affect, Visualize, and Enjoy). "To have it, you must TAVE it," was the slogan he taught.

Let's say that you don't want to forget the name of a person whom you've just met. (Let's suppose his name is William.) First create in your mind an image that you can easily associate with that person's name (For "William" you might visualize a sheet of paper labeled "Last <u>Will</u> & Testament, or perhaps a duck's <u>bill</u>, or maybe a windowed envelope containing your telephone <u>bill</u>, etc.) Next identify some aspect of the person's physical appearance that stands out in your mind. (Let's say he has a tiny scar on his chin.) Then you might imagine, for example, a duck's bill poking (Touching) the scar until it starts to bleed (Affecting it). The blood can appear as either liquid gold (if you perceive William as being a nice person

78    *Shades of Reality*

with a "heart of gold"), or green slime (if you don't like him). You must then concentrate on (Visualize) this mental scenario for a moment, and have fun Enjoying that image. If you carefully follow all of these steps, you will probably not only remember William's name whenever you see him again, but you will probably chuckle a little bit each time as well.

A technique that works well for memorizing numbers is to associate each digit with a different letter of the alphabet (or with a different spoken sound). By utilizing such a "phonetic alphabet" the meaningless digits in numbers can be converted into sequences of letters (or sounds) which can be associated with recognizable objects.

By utilizing tricks like the TAVE method along with the phonetic alphabet, it is possible to greatly improve your ability to recall almost any kind of information. (Since I've taken the memory class, my memory has become so good that I can't even recall the last time that I've ever *forgotten* anything!)

Perhaps we also need to make a distinction between *forgetting* and simply being *absentminded*. When a person becomes preoccupied with some activity, he/she may "forget" about previous commitments and obligations. This is not quite the same kind of forgetting as the "loss of recall" type of forgetting that we have been discussing (although absentmindedness also occurs in degrees). An absentminded person still *remembers* the information. But that information has simply been moved out of the "immediately active" area of his mind. (For example, do you remember your own telephone number? Of course you do. But I'll bet you weren't actively thinking about it until I brought it up.)

## Skill

Perhaps you are musically talented and know how to play a musical instrument. Almost everyone can manage to pick out at least one simple tune on a piano, even if they can only do so very clumsily and with just one finger. But would you say that such a

*Truth and Knowledge*    79

clumsy one-finger player "knows" how to play the piano? Probably not—at least not in the sense that we usually mean (i.e., that they're *skilled* at playing it).

Skill is similar to knowledge in that it represents acquired information (e.g., which piano keys correspond to which musical notes), but different in that it requires degrees of physical and mental dexterity as well. When all three of these aspects are developed together, we say that the person is skilled.

But mental dexterity is essentially knowledge at the subconscious level. The brain is "taught" to make connections between neurons that previously were not connected. These connections constitute patterns of information in the brain. Therefore, mental dexterity can also be regarded as a form of knowledge.

Let's return now to our one-finger piano player. She has just decided that it would be kind of fun to take some piano lessons. So after a couple of days of diligently practicing at the keyboard, she can eventually play a simple one-fingered tune almost all the way through without hardly making any mistakes at all. Does she *now* know how to play the piano?

Several more weeks pass and our piano student now knows a few simple chords. She even knows how to play some chords with her left hand while her right hand pounds out a simple melody. Would you say that she *now* knows how to play the piano?

How proficient must a person be before it can be said that he or she "knows" how to play the piano? How terribly must they play before they should be regarded as "not knowing" how to play. Is there anybody on earth who "completely knows" how to play the piano?

Clearly, skill is a matter of degree. Otherwise, everyone who "knows" how to play a musical instrument would be just as good as everyone else who "knows" how to play that instrument. But what exactly causes skill to be a matter of degree? If all knowledge were a bivalent all-or-nothing matter, then the only thing that would account for the existence of different degrees of skill would be the differences in degrees of physical dexterity.

80     *Shades of Reality*

Consider two virtually identical students. One student spends four years studying the piano. The other student is given absolutely no music lessons at all, but instead spends an equal amount of time exercising the very same finger, hand, and arm muscles that the first student is exercising by taking piano lessons.

After fourteen years the first student becomes a concert pianist. The only thing preventing the second student from being able to play the piano just as well should therefore be the missing knowledge of music. And so the second student could then become as equally good of a concert pianist as the first student, simply by reading music books to supply her with musical knowledge. Furthermore, if knowledge were all-or-nothing, there should be a well-defined *instant* in time at which she makes the transition from "not knowing" how to play the piano at all, to being a fully qualified concert pianist!

# Chapter Five

# Fallacy and Paradox

**Fallacy**

In studying high school algebra you may have come across "proofs" of mathematical absurdities, such as: $2 = 1$. Such a "proof" may have proceeded as follows:

        a)   Let $x = 1$

Squaring both sides of equation (a) yields –

        b)   $x^2 = 1^2 = 1$

Since $x = 1$ and $x^2 = 1$ we have –

        c)   $x^2 = x$

Subtracting one from both sides of equation (c) gives –

        d)   $x^2 - 1 = x - 1$

Factoring $x^2 - 1$ into $(x - 1)(x + 1)$ yields –

        e)   $(x - 1)(x + 1) = (x - 1)$

81

82      *Shades of Reality*

Canceling out the $(x - 1)$ term from both sides of the equation gives –

   f)   $(x + 1) = 1$

Substituting $x = 1$ from equation (a) produces –

   g)   $2 = 1$          Q.E.D.

Of course we know that 2 doesn't *really* equal 1, even though each step of our reasoning *seems* valid. And indeed upon further investigation we see that in going from equation (e) to equation (f) we discover that we *cannot* cancel out the $(x - 1)$ term. Since $x = 1$, then the term $(x - 1)$ is equal to zero. Therefore, if we try to cancel the $(x - 1)$ terms, we accidentally divided both sides of the equation by zero (which is a mathematical "no-no").

The above "proof" that 1 equals 2 is an example of what is known as a *fallacy*. In proving a fallacy you must commit one or more hidden mistakes (such as dividing by zero). When the mistake is finally discovered, you have a good chuckle at your misstep and you move on, secure in your understanding that the rules of mathematics are indeed consistent after all. If there had *not* been a misstep — if you had indeed discovered an actual inconsistency in the rules of arithmetic — your proof would have shaken the very foundations of mathematics! Such is the power and importance of consistency. (Recall our discussions about consistency, which were presented in Chapter Zero.)

**Paradox**

A logical paradox, like a fallacy, starts with a known fact and then proceeds, through a logical sequence of step-by-step reasoning, to arrive at a contradiction. But a paradox differs from a fallacy in at least one very important aspect — *a paradox has no hidden missteps.* Each step in the argument is valid. Logical paradoxes,

*Fallacy and Paradox*    83

therefore, are indications that there *is* something fundamentally wrong with the foundations of traditional logic!

## Sorites Paradox

We have already encountered and resolved one simple example of a paradox in our previous discussions — the sorites paradox of when does a heap of sand become a non-heap. Starting with a heap of sand you remove one grain and then ask the bivalent question, "Is it still a heap?" If so, you continue to remove one grain of sand at a time, each time asking for a 100 percent "yes" answer or a 100 percent "no" answer to the question "Is it still a heap"?

Fuzzy logic realizes that the correct answer to the question at each step is not an all-or-nothing "yes" or an all-or-nothing "no," but a degree of "yes" *and* "no." As each grain of sand is removed, the degree of "yes" *decreases* slightly and the degree of "no" *increases* slightly. Therefore, there is no grain of sand whose removal causes the answer to instantaneously jump from 100 percent "yes" to 100 percent "no."

An equivalent way of looking at the problem is to realize that the term "heap" is merely the name of a fuzzy set. Every pile of sand is (to some degree) a member of this set that we call "heap." As each grain of sand is removed, the resulting pile's membership value (in the "heap" set) gradually becomes less and less.

## Who Shaves the Barber?

The mathematician Bertrand Russell showed that the assumptions of crisp set theory could lead to contradiction and paradox. To illustrate, he imagined a small village in which a barber had a shop. On the window of his shop was the sign: "I shave all, and only, those men in the village who don't shave themselves." If the sign is true, then who shaves the barber? If he shaves himself, then his sign

## 84 *Shades of Reality*

says that he doesn't. And if he doesn't shave himself, then his sign says that he does!*

The Barber paradox is just one of many such paradoxes that can result when one tries to apply the all-or-nothing Aristotelian reasoning to statements of self-reference. And as amusing and trivial as they may seem, they actually reflect serious problems that arise in set theory when discussing sets that contain themselves. Specifically, if a set contains all (and only) those sets that don't contain themselves, does it contain itself? It can't — and yet, it must!

### Epimenides Paradox

Another example of self-reference is the famous Epimenides Paradox. Epimenides, who came from the island of Crete, supposedly once made the statement, "All Cretans are liars." If his statement was true, then it was false. And if it was false, then it was true.

As a slightly different version of the Epimenides Paradox, consider the following two statements:

a) Statement (b) is true.

b) Statement (a) is false.

Once again, if we assume that statement (a) is true, then we are immediately led to the conclusion that statement (a) is false. And if we assume that statement (a) is false, then statement (a) is true. But if we do not limit the scope of our assumptions to only extreme all-or-nothing truth — if we allow for the existence of *partial truth* — then we can conclude that both statements (a) and (b) are each *half true* and *half false*. (If we assume that statement (a) is 50 percent true, then statement (b) is only 50 percent true. This in turn makes statement (a) only 50 percent false, which is in complete agreement with our initial assumption.)

---

*An amusing "resolution" of this paradox is presented by Paul Sloane in his book, *Test Your Lateral Thinking IQ*. Mr. Sloane suggests that the barber is a *woman*!

*Fallacy and Paradox* **85**

As an aside, what if we were to change either one of the statements to its opposite? For example, suppose that we were to leave statement (a) unchanged, but change statement (b):

a) Statement (b) is true.

b) Statement (a) is true.

Now if we assume that statement (a) is true, we conclude that statement (a) *is* true. But what if we assume that statement (a) is *false*? Then, from statement (b), statement (a) *is* indeed false! So once again we see that:

**Statements of self-reference lead to only half-truths.**

## The Paradox of the Unexpected

As a final example of how fuzzy logic makes mincemeat out of paradox, consider the famous "paradox of the unexpected." There are many slightly different scenarios that have been used to express this paradox. One tells of a teacher who announces that there will be an unexpected exam sometime during the course of the semester. Another tells of an egg that has been hidden away inside one of ten numbered boxes, and if you open the boxes in numerical order you will not know in advance which box contains the egg. In each case the reasoning is exactly the same. So I will present:

## The Paradox of the Unexpected Execution

Once upon a time in a faraway kingdom there was a prisoner who had been sentenced to death. The king, who was an honest man and who never lied, paid a visit to the condemned prisoner. The king said to the man, "On one of the next seven days I am going to have you executed at sunset. I have already chosen the day, but there will be no way for you to determine which day it is. The day of your execution will come as a complete surprise to you. But if in

## 86     *Shades of Reality*

the morning of your execution day you can say to the jailer, 'This is the day the king has chosen,' then I have instructed him to set you free. But you are allowed only *one* such attempt." The king then walked away and left the prisoner to contemplate his fate.

The prisoner began to think. "Suppose that six of the seven days should pass and I have not yet been executed. Then the only day left would be the seventh day. And so I would know that this seventh day **must** be the day of my execution. But the king, who never lies, has told me that I would **not** be able to determine it. The day of my execution will come as a complete *surprise*. So I can completely eliminate day seven as a possibility. My execution will have to occur on one of the other **six** days."

And then the prisoner thought some more. "But suppose now that five days have come and gone and I'm still alive. Since I've been able to completely eliminate day seven as a possible execution day, that would leave only day six. And once again I would know the day of my execution as being day six. Therefore, I can eliminate day six too!"

Next he applied the same reasoning to day five and eliminated it as well by the very same arguments. Thinking through all the remaining days of the week the prisoner eventually came to the conclusion, "The king can't *ever* execute me without breaking his word." So he settled back, smug in the knowledge that he was safe.

But as the sun set on the third day, the king had the prisoner executed. And, true to the king's word, the execution *did* come as a complete surprise to the prisoner!

Before I present the resolution of this paradox, let me first point out that the king partially contradicted himself when he told the prisoner that the execution day would come as a *complete surprise*. It clearly cannot come as a *complete* surprise if the prisoner already knows that the execution will definitely occur on one of only seven upcoming days. The prisoner therefore "knew" the day of his execution to degree 1/7. And so the king was being only 6/7

*Fallacy and Paradox* 87

honest when he told the prisoner that there would be no way for him to determine the day. (Yes, even *honesty* occurs in degrees.) With each passing day, the degree to which the prisoner would know the day of his execution would steadily increase. On the second day he would know it to degree 1/6, on the third day to degree 1/5, . . . on the seventh day to degree 1 (i.e., to a certainty).

To understand the solution to the paradox let's imagine that this episode was not just a onetime event. Let's suppose that it was a standard policy of the king to make this very same offer to *every* condemned prisoner. Surely the king, himself, could have come to the conclusion that day 7 would have to be avoided as this would result in a certainty of having to free any prisoner who lasted that long. But if he *always* avoided day 7 *without exception*, then that fact would soon become common knowledge among the prisoners, and they would therefore be correct in eliminating day 7 as a possible execution day. In that case, the king would be "right back where he started" so to speak. Now he would have to avoid day *six* without exception, and this too would soon become common knowledge, etc. The downward trickle would continue until eventually there would be no more days for executions, and all prisoners would always be set free! This would make the king become a total liar, because he had explicitly stated that each execution *would* occur.

The king would therefore be caught between a rock and a hard place. No matter what he did, there would be no way for him to maintain the complete integrity of his statements to the prisoners. He would have to choose between being either a *total* liar or, at best, being only a *partial* liar. To maximize the degree of truthfulness of his statements, the king would not be able to exclude *any* day. Instead, he would have to randomly distribute the executions evenly over all of the days, including day 7. Of course this would mean that, on the average, 1/7 of the prisoners would always go free. But then we already knew that any prisoner could have just "taken a guess" at his execution day, and he would have had one chance in seven of being correct.

88 *Shades of Reality*

In summary, the paradox of the unexpected execution assumes that all of the king's statements are 100 percent true, and that the prisoner's knowledge of the execution day is 0 percent. These all-or-nothing assumptions are clearly incorrect. Instead, the king's statements about the unknowability of the execution day are only 6/7 true, and the prisoner's degree of knowledge of the execution day is 1/7. If the king had chosen to be completely honest, and to admit to the prisoner that he (the prisoner) *does* have this degree of knowledge, then there would no longer have been a paradox.

## Aristotelian Logic and Integers

In conclusion, a logical paradox can arise when all-or-nothing (i.e., *integer*) assumptions are made about an inherently fuzzy (i.e., *non-integer*) system. In this regard we can make the observation that:

> *Aristotelian logic is to integers,*
> *as fuzzy logic is to fractions.*

Suppose for a moment that mathematicians had developed modern day arithmetic with the same all-or-nothing guidelines that Aristotelian logic uses. (In fact ancient arithmetic *was* that way.) Such an "Aristotelian arithmetic" would therefore recognize the existence of only integer numbers. Concepts like fractions and irrational numbers would simply be unheard of (or at least not acknowledged as being anything more than maybe "the cocaine of mathematics").

Just think about the kinds of mathematical "paradoxes" that could arise inside such a framework! Values resulting from divisions would have to be rounded off to produce integer results. For example 5 divided by 3 would be perceived as being *exactly* equal to 2. And the number 1 divided by *any* number greater than zero could be perceived as being *either* 0 or 1. (The value could be perceived to be 1 since, as is often argued, "If any part of an entity

Fallacy and Paradox    89

exists then the *whole* entity exists." We will talk about this erroneous notion further when we discuss the concept of "drawing the line at zero" in the next chapter.)

In Aristotelian mathematics one would have, for example, the "paradox" that 6 equals 5:

$$5 / 3 = 5 / 3$$

Multiplying both sides by 3

$$3 (5 / 3) = 5$$

Since 5 / 3 is perceived to be identically equal to 2, we have

$$3 (2) = 5$$

or

$$6 = 5 \qquad \text{Q.E.D.}$$

It is important to understand that the above proof would represent a **paradox**, and *not* a **fallacy**. There were no hidden missteps in any part of its derivation. Instead, the problem lies in the *foundations* of such an Aristotelian mathematics. The paradox resulted from the failure of the Aristotelian system to recognize the existence of any kind of numerical values except for whole numbers. However, when we allow for "fuzzy integers" (like fractions), then the paradox of 6 = 5 no longer exists.

### Legal Paradoxes

Just as the sorites paradox (when does a heap become a non-heap?) exists in traditional logic, so too do similar paradoxes exist in the American legal system. (Where on the infinite continuum of possible human actions does *legal* turn into *illegal*? *Not* guilty into *guilty*?)

And just as logical paradoxes indicate that there is something fundamentally wrong with the foundations of traditional logic, so too

90     *Shades of Reality*

do *legal* paradoxes indicate that *there is something fundamentally wrong with the foundations of our legal system.* (The resolution of these paradoxes will constitute much of Part Two of this book.)

In addition it is possible to find other bizarre (and sometimes humorous) examples of other legal paradoxes.

### The "Becoming an Adult" Paradox

Several states (such as Texas, Florida, etc.) are sliced into two separate time zones. The western side of the state will be in one time zone, while the eastern side of the state will be in a time zone that is one hour later.

Imagine that you are a person living in one of these states, and that tomorrow is your twenty-first birthday. If you are living in the eastern part of the state and the clock strikes midnight, you will instantly become an adult of legal age. However, if you step west across the time zone line, you will not yet have become an adult, even though it is the very same "you" in the very same state! For one hour you would therefore legally *be* an adult in that state, and at the same time legally *not* be an adult!

Similarly, imagine two babies born one hour apart in time— the first one in New York at one o'clock A.M., and an hour later the second one in California. Because of the three hour time difference that exists between the east coast and the west coast, the California baby's time of birth will be eleven o'clock P.M. *of the previous day.* Twenty-one years later, the New Yorker is now living in California. However, he will not legally become an adult until *tomorrow*, even though he is actually *older* than his native Californian counterpart who is already an adult *today*!

### The "O.J. Simpson" Paradox

(This paradox is not specifically unique to the O. J. Simpson case. However, because of the national press coverage of the trials, it represents the most well-known example.)

*Fallacy and Paradox*     91

Imagine you are sitting quietly at home in your living room when suddenly a baseball comes smashing through your front window. You get up, look outside, and you see a boy with a baseball glove standing on the sidewalk in front of your house. You accuse the boy of breaking your window. But just then your neighbors come out and testify that the boy *didn't* break your window. He just happened to be passing by. It was actually some other boy who broke your window, and he ran away. So you say to the boy, "OK, so you didn't break my window. But I'm still going to make you pay for it *anyway!*"

This is essentially what has happened in the O. J. Simpson verdicts. When O. J. Simpson was placed on trial for murder, the jury found him to be not guilty. In effect, the American legal system declared that he did not commit the murders. And yet the same legal system, in Simpson's civil trial, found him *liable* for those murders.

Whether or not he *actually* committed the crimes is not the issue here. *Legally*, he did not commit the crimes (even if he *actually* did). And yet he was legally required to pay for those crimes that he allegedly did not commit!

Legal professionals try to weasel out of this paradox by explaining that a criminal trial is not intended to prove actual guilt or non-guilt of the defendant. Instead, the results of a criminal trial merely reflect how well the attorneys were able to present their respective cases. But then, if this is so, our legal system is admittedly not looking for *truths*. Instead, its only goal is to deliver a verdict that is based solely on how well each side "*plays the game.*" (We will have more to say about the "game" of law in Chapter Eight.)

### "Truth, Justice, and the American Way"

To make matters even worse the American legal system has declared that, once a person's attorneys "win the game" for him, he cannot be put on trial again for the same crime (double jeopardy). After being acquitted of the crime, the defendant could even brag

## 92    *Shades of Reality*

about how he got away with it, if he so chooses, and no further legal recourse could be made against him. Even after the *real* truth became known, the *legal* "truth" would still remain "not guilty." Our system of law says, in effect: "My mind is made up, so don't confuse me with the facts." That is the American way!

If science (which *does* look for real truth) were to be conducted with the same philosophy that governs our legal system, then scientists would be prohibited from making any new discoveries that might conflict with results that were achieved in previous experiments. For example when I was working on the Apollo Lunar Sounder Experiment project at the Jet Propulsion Laboratory back in the 1970s, we failed to detect the presence of any water on the moon. However, recent findings by the Clementine spacecraft (1997) indicate the possible existence of water ice in the lunar polar regions.

Should we now reject this new evidence of water simply because it had already been shown back in the 1970s that water *doesn't* exist on the moon? Should science adopt a policy that would prevent such "double jeopardy" of established results? Of course not. Because in science (unlike in law) *reality* is the name of the game. And reality is just too powerful a concept to let itself be conveniently swept under a rug of self-imposed ignorance.

As we saw in the "Introduction To Reality" at the beginning of this book, our perceptions of the truths of the universe are constantly changing. When looking for the *truths* of reality, it is essential to always keep an open mind and be constantly prepared to re-evaluate any new data which may become available. If the American legal system ever decides to partake in a similar search for *real* truths (instead of its *make-believe* "truths"), then it too must be prepared to re-evaluate new evidence whenever it becomes available. To do otherwise is to reject reality in favor of fantasy, and to continue to provide an open invitation to paradox.

# Chapter Six

# Fuzzy Words and Fuzzy Existence

As we mentioned in Chapter two, the human mind has the ability to form generalized concepts from specific occurrences. For example we can look at two different oak trees and, even though they may be of different sizes and have completely different shapes in their branches, we still recognize and categorize them by using the word, "tree." Even a completely different type of tree, such as an evergreen tree, is still recognized as being in the category called "tree." Words such as "tree" therefore represent a kind of shorthand notation for summarizing all of the separate occurrences of such similar plants.

But if you plant an acorn, is it immediately a "tree?" When it first begins to sprout, is it then a "tree"? Which things are properly described by the word, "tree," and which things are not? Words, like "tree," have an imprecision about them. There is no clear-cut distinction between "tree" and "non-tree." Therefore, words like "tree" represent fuzzy sets.

But nouns aren't the only words that are fuzzy. Adjectives too can have vagueness to them. For example we can speak of a "big" tree, or a "red" apple, or a "good" person. But where is the

93

## 94     Shades of Reality

boundary between "big" and "little," between "red" and some other color, or between "good" and "bad"? Just how bad does a person have to be before he can no longer be referred to as being a "good" person? (As the old saying goes, "There's a little bit of bad in the best of us, and a little bit of good in the worst of us.") The answer is, there isn't any threshold line. Instead, a person's "goodness" is measured by his or her membership value in the fuzzy set called "good persons."

However, not *all* words are fuzzy. Consider for example the adjective, "five," as in "five trees." While there may be a degree of vagueness associated with the word, "trees," there is nothing vague about the word, "five." (I don't mean "four," and I don't mean "six.") Since words are merely a shorthand way of expressing concepts, if a concept (such as "five-ness") is crisp, then so too will be the word corresponding to the concept.

Let's briefly take a look at some commonly used fuzzy words and phrases and see how they are generally given incorrect crisp interpretations.

### Proximity: "Near" and "Far"

As has been pointed out many times in these first several chapters, there is a human propensity to try to collapse the real world into perfectly straight lines and points. For example on a road atlas, most of the cities and towns are represented as single black dots, not because the towns are too small to be seen as identifiable shapes on the map, but simply because we *think* in terms of points.

Look at the three "objects" (dots) shown in Figure 6.1. Which of the two end objects (**a** or **b**) is nearer to the center object, **c**? Which one is farther away from **c**?

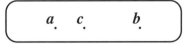

Figure 6.1

## Fuzzy Words and Fuzzy Existence        95

The answer of course is: **a** is closer and **b** is farther away. (In fact **a** is almost twice as close to **c** as **b** is.)

But now look at the three objects shown in Figure 6.2. Which of the two objects, **a** or **b**, is closer to the object, **c**? Which of the two objects is farther away from **c**?

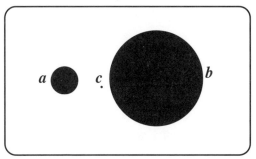

Figure 6.2

Now you would probably answer that **b** is closer and that **a** is farther away, even though the *center* of each object is *identical* to the "centers" of the objects shown in Figure 6.1.

When objects have non-zero size (i.e., when they are bigger than points), there seems to be an unwritten convention mandating that distances be determined by using only the very *closest two points* on each of the objects. Why these two somewhat arbitrary points should be the sole determiners of distance is a mystery to me.

In fact one can argue that object **b** is both nearer *and* farther away than is object **a**! Because there exist points (on the left side of object **b**) that are *closer* to point **c** than are any of the points on object **a**. And at the same time there also exist points (on the right side of object **b**) that are *farther* away from **c** than are any of the points on object **a**!

This leads to one of those amusing contradictions that fuzzy logic is so famous for:

$$b < a$$

96     *Shades of Reality*

while at the same time,

$$b > a.$$

Of course these inequalities are only true to some degree. And the degree to which they are true is determined by the fraction of the objects' areas for which the inequalities are valid.

### "I've Been There"

One of the activities I enjoy doing the most is traveling. In 1989 I bought a little motor home and drove it all over the United States and Canada. In fact I've driven it through every Canadian province and every state in the U.S. except for Hawaii. (I've been to Hawaii several times but never in the motor home — too damp trying to get there!) So am I now qualified to claim that "I have been in every state in the United States?"

Let's pretend that you are a native Californian and that you've never been outside of the state. But someday you would like to be able to make the claim of having "been in every state in the country." So you set out on your first trip — an excursion along what is left of old historic Route 66, the famous highway that used to connect Los Angeles (or more precisely, Santa Monica) with Chicago.

Starting at Ocean Avenue in Santa Monica you head east along Santa Monica Boulevard, carefully following your Route 66 maps and guidebooks. (In many areas the old road no longer exists, and so you must take detours to follow the *approximate* route.) After driving about 200 miles through Los Angeles, San Bernardino, Barstow, and Needles, you eventually cross over the Colorado River to reach your first "new" state, Arizona.

After driving across Arizona for about 350 miles (of mostly desert), you eventually cross the state line into New Mexico (where you get to see another 350 miles of mostly desert!)

Next you reach the Texas panhandle, and after driving about

*Fuzzy Words and Fuzzy Existence*     97

another 175 miles (and passing through Amarillo) you arrive in your fourth new state, Oklahoma.

Once again you have another 350 miles of driving to do (taking you through Oklahoma City and Tulsa) before you reach your next new state, Kansas.

Now, Kansas is kind of unique in respect to Route 66 — there are only about 12 miles of the road there. The route just barely passes through the southeast corner of the state before reaching the Missouri state line. (Once in Missouri, you will again have to travel hundreds of miles before you reach the final state for Route 66, Illinois.) So, having traveled through these 12 miles of Kansas, is it really fair to say that you have now "been in Kansas?"

If you had simply reached across the Kansas state line with your little finger and then turned around and went back home, would that too have counted as "being in Kansas?" If after returning from such a trip you were to tell one of your friends, "I was in Kansas," and you offered no further words of explanation, would your claim match your friend's perception of what really happened?

If a statement conveys a high degree of misinformation, then that statement must have a high degree of *falseness* associated with it. Therefore, the expression, "I've been to somewhere," is true only to some degree, and false to some degree. And the degree of *falseness* is determined by how much of the "somewhere" that you *haven't* been to. (When viewed in this perspective, *nobody* has ever been much of *anywhere*!)

Even the claim that you traveled on old Route 66 is only partly true. Since most of the actual asphalt for the road no longer exists (or has been paved over with *new* asphalt), what exactly does the expression, "being on Route 66," mean? Does it count if you're merely in the general vicinity of the former road? And if so, then just how far away can you get before you are *no longer* on Route 66? Or you might even turn the question around slightly and ask, "How much of your trip was *not* spent on Route 66?" And even more to the point, "How much of the *entire* Route 66 did you *miss*

98     *Shades of Reality*

traveling on" (either because you took side excursions, or simply because parts of the original road no longer exist)?

All claims of having "been" somewhere are fuzzy. For example have you ever "been" to your own *hometown*? There are many places even there that you have never been (for example, a restaurant in which you've never eaten, or an alley that you've never walked through, or the bathroom in a stranger's house on the other side of town).

### "On" and "Off"

Imagine an ordinary electric lightbulb connected to a simple on/off switch. When the switch is in the "on" position, the lightbulb glows at full brilliance, and we say that the lightbulb is "on." When the switch is in the "off" position, no electricity flows, and so we say that the lightbulb is "off."

But now imagine the same lightbulb connected to a dimmer switch. When the switch is set to its maximum setting, the lightbulb once again glows at its full brilliance. When the switch is set to its minimum setting, no electricity flows. When the switch is set to any intermediate setting, the lightbulb glows with an intermediate level of brightness that is linearly proportional to the setting.

Assume that the dimmer switch initially starts out at its *minimum* setting. And then, over a period of one minute, the switch slowly and uniformly moves to its *maximum setting. When does the lightbulb go on?*

Whenever I ask anybody this question, the answers they give are almost always the same: "The lightbulb goes on the instant the switch starts moving. Because the bulb has to be considered as being "on" if even so much as *one* electron starts flowing through it."

Then I reverse the question. I start the dimmer switch at the *maximum* setting and let it move toward the *minimum* setting. When I ask: "When does the lightbulb go *off*"? the answers are again

*Fuzzy Words and Fuzzy Existence*     99

unanimous: "The lightbulb doesn't go off until the switch reaches the minimum position and all of the electricity *stops* flowing."

But there is a fundamental inconsistency to their reasoning. If the term "going on" is to be interpreted as making the transition from an extreme state (no electricity flowing) to a non-extreme state (a small amount of electricity *beginning* to flow), then by symmetrical reasoning, the term "going off" should mean making the transition from an extreme state (maximum electricity flowing) to a non-extreme state (a small amount of electricity *ceasing* its flow). In other words if "going on" means leaving the *minimum* setting, then "going off" should mean leaving the *maximum* setting.

For example instead of having a dimmer switch that changes the *brightness* of a lightbulb, imagine one that somehow changes its *color*. Let's say that when the switch is at its minimum setting the bulb is **red**. But as the switch moves to its maximum setting, the color of the bulb smoothly changes to **blue**. Therefore, **red** corresponds to "off" in our previous discussion, and **blue** corresponds to "on." If I now ask the completely equivalent question: "When does the bulb go **blue**"? Would the answer still be that it happens at the instant the switch leaves its minimum position because "the presence of even the slightest amount of blueness makes the bulb **blue**"? And if so, then how about the second question: "When does the bulb go **red**"? Would the answer still be that the bulb doesn't go **red** until the switch is all the way back to its minimum position and all of the blueness is gone? It seems to me that if the presence of even a small amount of blueness justifies calling the bulb **blue**, then the same reasoning should be valid for **red** as well.

**Drawing the Line at Zero**

By now we should realize that a lightbulb on a dimmer switch doesn't just go "on" or "off" (or **blue** or **red**) at a specified point. Instead, at any setting of the switch, the lightbulb is always "on" to some degree, and also "off" to some degree. Therefore, my

100    *Shades of Reality*

question, "When does the lightbulb go on"? was intentionally mis-worded (since some degree of "on"-ness exists at *every* position of the dimmer switch). But our discussion about the common interpretation of the word "on" illustrates the traditional notion that if *any part* of an entity exists (such as "on"-ness), then the entity *totally* exists. (This same notion was also manifested in our former example of claiming to have "been in Kansas" simply by virtue of having been in any part of Kansas.) I refer to this mind-set as: **drawing the line at zero**. We will see more examples of this peculiar mind-set, particularly in Part Two of this book.

### To Be, Or Not To Be?

Place a small chunk of dry ice on an empty table inside of a warm room, and then leave for several hours. Chances are when you return to the room, the dry ice will have completely sublimed, and the table will once again be empty.

*At what point in time did the chunk of dry ice cease to exist?*

This question might seem like nothing more than a warmed-over version of the sorites paradox of the heap. But there is at least one important, albeit subtle, distinction. The heap paradox looked for the point of transition between two *existing* entities (i.e., a cluster of sand grains called a "heap" vs. a cluster of sand grains *not* called a "heap"). The question about the dry ice takes the matter even further and raises the question about the boundary line between *existence* and *non-existence*.

You might want to argue that the chunk of dry ice *never did* cease to exist. Its molecules are still there, but now they exist as a gas instead of a solid. But then a similar objection could also be raised about the heap paradox — each of the removed particles of sand is still there *too*, only in a different location.

Next, you might be tempted to claim that the chunk of dry ice ceased to exist when it became too small to be seen. But too small

*Fuzzy Words and Fuzzy Existence*     101

to be seen *how*? With the naked eye? With a magnifying glass? With a microscope? Where do you "draw the line" between visible and *not* visible? Of course you could just choose some arbitrary size, like maybe the wavelength of light, and declare *that* to be the limit of seeability. But to what avail? Only an ostrich would think that something is really *gone* just because it can't be *seen*.

And so you eventually "draw the line at zero" and claim that the chunk of dry ice continued to exist until its size reached "zero" (i.e., the exact instant at which its very last molecule of carbon dioxide sublimated). At that precise moment in time it instantly changed from the category called "existing," into the category called "*not* existing."

But we already know from the Smoothness Principle that no such exact time can be determined. Besides, there were probably many carbon dioxide molecules in the air near the surface of the table, even *before* you brought the chunk of dry ice into the room. Would you call each of *those* molecules "chunks of dry ice" too?

**Degrees of Existence**

The English language has many words for expressing comparative gradations of certain concepts. For example, "colder," "cooler," "warmer," "hotter," etc. all describe degrees of temperature (no pun intended). And words like "tinier," "smaller," "larger," etc. all describe degrees of size. But there are no words like "iser" and "isn'ter" (i.e., more than or less than "is" and "isn't") for describing degrees of *existence*. Such words don't exist because the *concept* of degrees of existence doesn't exist (until now!). To our all-or-nothing mentalities, existence either *is*, or else it *isn't*. There is nothing in between those two possibilities. Something either *exists* — or else it *doesn't*. Period!

When it comes to matters about existence, we "*draw the line at zero*." On the "above zero" side of the line is total *existence*. On the other side is total *non-existence*. But if "everything is a matter of

102     *Shades of Reality*

degree," as the fuzzy principle states, then what are the degrees of *existence*?

## An Old Riddle

At one time or another in your life you've probably had somebody ask you the following riddle (or some version of it):

> If it takes three men four hours to dig a hole, then
> how long will it take one man to dig half of a hole?

Upon first hearing the riddle you probably did a little arithmetic — the number of man-hours required was 3 times 4, which is 12. So it should take half that long (6 hours) for a single person to dig half of the hole.

> "Six hours," was your answer.
> "Wrong!" exclaimed the riddler. "There's no such thing as a half of a hole!"

Conventional logic dictates that holes exist all-or-nothing. The instant you remove the first shovelful of dirt, you *immediately* have a hole — a *whole* hole.

For our purposes, a hole can be regarded as being an *anti-heap* (and likewise, a heap can be regarded as being an *anti-hole*.) And if you start digging the hole on level ground, you will create *both* simultaneously. Every grain of sand that comes out of the hole will go to form part of the heap. And when the time comes to fill in the hole, the heap and the hole will annihilate each other to once again produce level ground. In fact, if there *were* such a word as "isn'ter," you might say that a hole *isn'ter* a heap! (If a "non-existent heap" refers to almost level ground, then a hole would be a heap that has even *less* than *non-existence*!)

By symmetry, any arguments about heaps should also apply to

*Fuzzy Words and Fuzzy Existence*     103

their *anti* counterparts, holes. If a heap is a fuzzy concept, then a hole is a fuzzy concept.

Consider now the fuzzy set of all "holes." Every depression in the ground is therefore a member of this set to some degree. Even a mere dent has some small degree of "hole-ness" to it. Imagine starting with such a dent and gradually pounding it more and more concave until its membership value in the set of "holes" just equals 1/2. Couldn't this depression in the ground be legitimately interpreted as being "half of a hole"?

**Other Examples of Partial Existence**

Besides dry ice and holes, what other kinds of things might have degrees of existence? (Actually, *everything* has a degree of existence. But the degree is often 100 *percent*!)

Let's return to our question about when the sky gets dark. At any point in time the question, "To what degree is the sky dark"? has an answer that lies in the range 0 percent to 100 percent, depending on *how dark it is*. But this simply means that, at any point in time*, darkness exists to some degree.* (And, at any point in time, *daylight* also exists to some degree.)

Next, consider the *alternate* form of the same question. "Is it dark yet"? can be answered by "yes" to some degree, and "no" to some degree. But this merely implies that "yes" *partially exists* in the answer, and "no" *partially exists* in the answer. In fact *any* question that requires a degree of "yes" and a degree of "no" in its answer implies partial existence of each of these two components.

As we have already seen, *truth* is a matter of degree. Therefore, any statement is only true to some degree. But once again, this simply means that truth only *partially exists* in the statement.

**Electrons**

One of the best examples of partial existence comes from the field of atomic physics.

104     *Shades of Reality*

Around 1920 the Danish physicist, Niels Bohr, fostered the belief that the electrons of an atom were tiny negatively charged particles that revolved around the positively charged nucleus (in much the same manner that the planets of our solar system orbit the sun).

In 1923 the French physicist Louis de Broglie suggested that electrons (and all subatomic particles) had the properties of waves, and in 1927 experiments were performed that showed him to be correct.

Around the same time, the German physicist Erwin Schrodinger had developed a model of the atom in which all of its particles were viewed as consisting of tiny packets of waves.

Today, the atom is no longer viewed as a nucleus surrounded by *orbiting* electrons, but as a nucleus surrounded by an electron *cloud*. Until quite recently this "cloud" (which is essentially the solution of Schrodinger's wave equation) was regarded as indicating the *probability* of finding the electron at each particular point in the atom. But the view currently coming into acceptance is that the electron cloud is **not** a *probability* distribution, but the *actual* distribution. Each electron therefore partially exists *everywhere* around the nucleus, but *its degree of existence* is a function of location.

### Anti-Aliasing

As another example, consider the very concept of "shades of gray." "Gray" represents nothing more than the *partial existence* of "black" and the *partial existence* of "white." In fact this forms the basis for a computer graphics technique known as "anti-aliasing."

One of the problems with trying to draw a black and white line in low resolution computer graphics is that if the line has only a gentle slope, the resulting image becomes a series of noticeable "stair steps," (see Figure 6.3). This is because each pixel in the image is either a black pixel or a white pixel. (Either a dot of light *exists* on the computer screen, or else it *doesn't* exist on the screen.)

*Fuzzy Words and Fuzzy Existence* 105

Figure 6.3

But if we allow for partial existence of pixels (i.e., pixels which are not just on or off, but shades of gray in between), then it is possible to produce a line in which the visual effect of the stair steps is reduced. An example of such an *anti-aliased* line is shown in Figure 6.4. (Stand back several feet and compare Figure 6.4 with Figure 6.3.)

Figure 6.4

**Conclusion**

At first, the concept of something only "partially existing" might have seemed like an impossibility. But when viewed in the proper perspective, it becomes quite understandable. In fact we can now see that the entire concept of existence can be viewed equivalently in a number of different ways. For example if a lightbulb (or a pixel, etc.) is "on" to some degree (let's say, 30 percent) then we can make the following equivalent statements:

- The lightbulb is "on" to degree 30 percent
- The light from the bulb "exists" to degree 30 percent
- The bulb's "on"-ness has a 30 percent degree of existence

## 106    *Shades of Reality*

- The 30 percent level of light from the bulb has 100 percent existence

- The 60 percent level of light from the bulb has 50 percent existence

- The light is "off" to degree 70 percent

- Darkness exists to degree 70 percent

etc.

In closing, let me just point out that *intangibles* (like "good," "evil," "pain," "happiness," etc.) can now be viewed in terms of having only partial existence (or existence to some degree) at any point in time. For example, saying that a person is experiencing "minor pain" is essentially equivalent to saying *either* that "partial pain" exists, or that pain "partially exists." For all practical purposes both are synonymous.

However, when dealing with *tangibles* (like an apple), the concept of partial existence becomes somewhat vague. A half of an apple is not quite the same thing as a whole apple that only half-exists. (Perhaps half-existence of a whole apple would result in some kind of "ethereal" apple that you can't quite get your hands on.) But in another sense, a half of an apple *is* an apple that only partially exists. (After all, the *whole* apple *isn't* there.) It's kind of a matter of semantics. It's kind of fuzzy.

Part Two

# The Social Implications of the Fuzzy Paradigm

# The Kingdom of Aristotelia

Far away on the western shores of the great Absurdian Sea lies the little-known kingdom of Aristotelia. Though peaceful and serene today, its history had long been marred by many, and often bloody, boundary disputes.

Aristotelians had always demanded the establishment of clear-cut and simple boundary lines with the neighboring countries. But none of the Absurdian principalities could ever seem to agree on an equitable boundary system.

In 1721 King Huffinpout III decided to settle the boundary issue once and for all by simply confiscating all of the Absurdian principalities and unifying them in the name of the Crown. But after several months of heavy fighting, his troops were finally repelled, and King Huffinpout III abdicated the throne.

"If I can't get it _all_, Then I don't want _nothin'_"! he declared as he fled into exile. But his famous "_All-or-Nothing_" speech had had a profound effect on the Aristotelian parliament, and even now still represents the principal guideline governing the policies of the kingdom.

*The Kingdom of Aristotelia*     109

Today, Aristotelia is a modern and industrialized country, although some of its technologies and philosophies might be regarded as somewhat strange, especially by American standards. For example Aristotelian cameras do not work properly with color film, as they are designed to record only black and white images with no shades of gray.

Similarly, Aristotelian-built automobiles (which come in your choice of either black or white) have gas gauges that indicate only FULL or EMPTY, and speedometers that indicate only MOVING or STOPPED.

In the kitchen, Aristotelian ovens have only two settings: OFF and HOT. Consequently, all food in the kingdom is eaten either raw or burned.

Aristotelian clocks display time only as DAY or NIGHT. Because when the day comes to an end in Aristotelia, there isn't any gradual period of *twilight* — it just suddenly becomes *totally dark*!

The Aristotelian educational system, which is run by the Aristotelian Academic Administration (or AAA, not to be confused with the Aristotelian Automobile Association), is the finest in the land. All students in the kingdom are required by law to attend the Aristotelian Royal Majesty's Provincial Institute of Technology, affectionately known as ARMPIT. There they are instructed in the "All-or-Nothing" philosophies of old King Huffinpout III.

Upon completion of their studies, each student is given a grade of "pass" or "fail." Those students who *pass* come out of ARMPIT smelling like a rose, for they now know absolutely *everything* there is to know! On the other hand, those students who *fail* are promptly expelled from ARMPIT, and they become the dregs of society who are *totally* uneducated and who know absolutely nothing about *anything*.

When an Aristotelian finishes school and joins the workforce, he receives the same salary as any other graduate, regard-

110    *Shades of Reality*

less of the type of job or the number of hours he has to work. Similarly, all non-graduates are paid absolutely *nothing* for their labors, since they are obviously not qualified to *do* anything.

Farming in Aristotelia is one of the most hazardous professions in the kingdom. When an Aristotelian farmer plants seeds, they don't just slowly germinate into seedlings. Instead, fully grown plants *instantly* shoot up out of the ground, hurling rocks and dirt for hundreds of miles in all directions. Because of the danger, the Aristotelian Aviation Agency (or AAA, not to be confused with the Aristotelian Academic Administration) prohibits commercial aircraft from flying over agricultural regions during the planting season. Furthermore the Aristotelian Academy of Astronomers (or AAA, not to be confused with the Aristotelian Aviation Agency) has speculated that many of the meteors that appear each August in the annual Perseid meteor shower are actually just bits and pieces of Aristotelian farmland reentering the earth's atmosphere.

Because all forms of plant and animal life emerge instantly and fully developed in Aristotelia, the kingdom has no need for abortion clinics or pediatricians. Immediately upon *conception* a newborn Aristotelian instantly emerges as a *fully-grown adult*. Therefore, it is not at all uncommon for an Aristotelian man to go to bed with a woman and wake up the next morning to find himself in bed with *two* women!

In the area of fine art, Aristotelian painters rank among the finest in the world. Who among us has never seen the immortal masterpiece, "Polar Bears in a Snow Storm," or the majestically beautiful, "Coal Mine at Midnight?" And in the field of music, Aristotelian musicians are in a class by themselves. In fact almost every household in the kingdom has an Aristotelian piano in its parlor, and even the little children have become quite proficient at repeatedly pressing down on its one and only key.

In April of each year the Association of Aristotelian Artists (or AAA, not to be confused with the Aristotelian Academy of

*The Kingdom of Aristotelia*     111

Astronomers) broadcasts its national music competition in search of new and talented Aristotelian musicians. In 1912 the grand prize was awarded to a strange and wondrously beautiful new piece of music that had suddenly appeared on the radio. But it was later discovered that the music was merely a distress call from the S. S. Titanic. (··· --- ··· - ·· ·- -· ·· -·-)

In the area of athletic competition, Aristotelian athletes are consistent winners. In the 100-meter dash, for example, the winner is everybody who crosses the finish line, regardless of who gets there *first*. In this way, *everyone* has an equal chance of winning, and the *faster* runners don't have an unfair advantage over the *slower* ones. As unbelievable as it may seem, almost every Aristotelian athlete who has ever competed in the 100-meter dash has *won* — all except for Harvey Klutz back in the Summer Games of 1937.

There had been an unusual amount of inclement weather that year, and the start of the 100-meter dash had to be delayed until late afternoon because of an unexpected thunder storm. When the weather finally cleared up and the beautiful black and white rainbow appeared in the Aristotelian sky, the track officials once again prepared to start the race.

The starting gun was fired, and the contestants were off and running! But just then the sun went down, and the sudden darkness caught poor Harvey Klutz in mid-stride. Before he could slow down, Harvey accidentally ran into a tree and had to be carried away on a stretcher. The other contestants, however, all had the foresight to tie little flashlights onto their shoes in the event of just such an emergency. So all of those "light-footed" runners succeeded in *finishing* the race.

Aristotelian Pole Vaulting is also an equally exciting event. The Aristotelian Athletic Association (or AAA, not to be confused with the Association of Aristotelian Artists) draws a thin white line on the ground with a piece of chalk, and the contestants are required to pole vault over it without knocking it down.

112    *Shades of Reality*

Once again, every Aristotelian athlete who has ever competed in pole vaulting has been fantastically successful at it!

The Aristotelian all-or-nothing mentality also governs the kingdom's judicial system. When a person is placed on trial for a crime, a jury declares him to be either *totally* guilty, or else he's found to be not guilty *at all*.

An Aristotelian reaches "legal age" at the moment of his twenty-first birthday. At that precise instant in time he suddenly becomes as equally mature and wise as every other adult in the kingdom — except, of course, for those citizens who are over thirty-five years of age. Because the moment that an Aristotelian turns thirty-five, he once again receives a *second* jolt of new wisdom and maturity, and can then run for the office of *King* if he so chooses.

And when *voting* for a new king, each Aristotelian *over* the age of eighteen gets exactly *one whole vote* — while each Aristotelian *under* the age of eighteen gets absolutely *no vote at all*.

I don't know about you, but after hearing about the Aristotelian way of life it sure makes *me* proud to be an *American*, where we would never even *think* of doing *any* of those kinds of stupid things!

*The Kingdom of Aristotelia*    113

# *Warning!*

Most of what we will discuss in the rest of this book is a direct extension of the materials that we have already covered in Part One. Yet my past experience has shown me that even those individuals who claim to understand the fundamentals of fuzzy logic and the concept of shades of gray still have trouble extending those ideas into real life. The current social norms and the 2000 year old Aristotelian all-or-nothing mentality are barriers that are just too strong for most Americans to overcome. So I am warning you now that many readers will find it difficult to understand some of the concepts that will be developed, not because the concepts are intrinsically difficult, but simply because those concepts are not "the American way." I would therefore strongly suggest that you now take the time to go back and reread any sections of Part One that you may be "fuzzy" about. Because if you don't understand them, you will most certainly disagree with just about everything to come.

# Chapter Seven

# Fuzzy Logic in the Real World

If this book were like most of the current books on fuzzy logic, we would now begin to show how the ideas developed in Part One can be applied to electrical engineering problems. In fact it is in the field of engineering that fuzzy logic has, to date, enjoyed its greatest development and application.

As a textbook example of the application of fuzzy logic to engineering, one could design a "fuzzy air conditioner." Such a device would utilize a *range* of values for the speed of the compressor motor, instead of using just the two extreme speeds (either running full blast, or being totally off). An air conditioner with a motor whose speeds are "shades of gray" between "on" and "off" would be able to maintain a constant room temperature better. Conventional air conditioners must first wait for the room temperature to exceed the maximum thermostat setting, at which point they blast the room with cold air until the minimum setting on the thermostat is reached. This means that the temperature in the room must swing from a bit too hot to a bit too cold. A fuzzy air conditioner on the other hand could keep it "just right."

*Fuzzy Logic in the Real World* **115**

The application of fuzzy logic to engineering is not just a theory or a hypothetical possibility of what it might someday be possible to do. Fuzzy logic is *already* in everyday use, particularly in Japan.

The Japanese city of Sendai has a subway system that is probably the most advanced in the world. The subway train moves so smoothly that standing passengers don't even need to hold on to poles or straps. A fish tank could travel the entire 8.4 mile route, stop at all 16 stations, and never even spill a drop of water. The subway is, of course, controlled by fuzzy logic.

Matsushita Electric Industrial Company (known in the United States as Panasonic, Quasar, and Technics) is the world's largest manufacturer of consumer electronics. In 1990 Masushita introduced a washing machine as the first major consumer appliance to incorporate fuzzy logic. The machine would sense the size of the load and the amount of dirt, and automatically adjust the wash cycle accordingly.

Matsushita (as well as Hitachi) also makes a fuzzy vacuum cleaner that uses an infrared sensor to measure the amount of dust on the floor. The machine then automatically sets the proper level of suction by adjusting the speed of the motor.

Matsushita and Sanyo also make fuzzy rice cookers. (No, they don't cook "fuzzy rice.") These rice cookers allow the user to select between four different kinds of cooked rice: hard, medium, soft, and sushi. Each type requires a different amount of water and a different steaming method. But by utilizing fuzzy logic, the user can simply fill the cooker to a single water level and the device automatically makes the adjustments.

Sanyo, Toshiba, and Sharp all make fuzzy microwave ovens, which sense temperature and humidity, and automatically adjust the cooking power and time. Normally, microwave ovens are either totally "on" (cooking) or totally "off" (not cooking) at any instant of time while they are in operation. (If you set the oven to less than full power and listen carefully, you can actually

116    *Shades of Reality*

hear when it goes on and off.) By allowing for intermediate values of "on-ness" more uniform cooking can be achieved.

In what might be considered to be almost the supreme oxymoron, Canon has come out with something called "fuzzy focus!" Traditional self-focusing cameras would simply bounce an infrared (or ultrasound) signal off of whatever single object was at the dead center of the field of view and then use that information to determine the distance. But if there were two or more objects present, such auto-focusing cameras could get confused. Canon solved the problem by allowing the camera to consider multiple targets and, utilizing fuzzy logic, incorporates them all.

In 1990 Matsushita introduced a fuzzy camcorder that automatically reduces the amount of jitter caused by handheld operation. (Several months later, *Fortune* named it a Product of the Year.) It is possible to eliminate the jitter by identifying the difference between motion *inside* the view (such as a person waving his hands) and motion of the view *as a whole* (where the entire frame shifts vertically or horizontally as a single unit). To distinguish between these two different types of motions, Matsushita used fuzzy logic to develop what it called a "digital image stabilizer." The stabilizer compares each pair of successive frames to see how much they have shifted, and then adjusts them accordingly.

Also in 1990, Fujitsu announced that it had developed a fuzzy electronic "eye" that could distinguish three-dimensional physical objects and even calculate their speeds of motion. The fuzzy eye has been successfully used in tests of automatically driven automobiles, and those vehicles were driven around corners and past obstacles without collisions.

Even elevators are becoming fuzzy. Companies such as Otis are working on the development of smart elevators — devices that employ fuzzy logic to adjust to the level of traffic. By knowing how many passengers are currently in each elevator, which floors have passengers waiting to board, and the locations

*Fuzzy Logic in the Real World*     117

of all of the elevators currently in use, an optimum strategy of operation can be dynamically achieved.

Day by day, the concept of fuzzy logic is becoming more and more a part of modern engineering. In fact fuzzy logic is starting to become so commonly used in engineering that most engineers who utilize the fuzzy concept actually think that "fuzzy logic" pertains *only* to "electrical circuits"!

We can now venture into the relatively unexplored areas of how fuzzy logic can be applied to the *non*-electrical everyday world. Let's begin by examining the part of the world where the concepts of vagueness and contradiction have already been accepted for thousands of years.

## Eastern Philosophy

Many concepts in Eastern philosophy arose in India and China, and have had little expression in the Western world.

Jainism is an ancient religion which, by some accounts, has origins dating as far back as 2500 B.C. Daniel McNeill and Paul Freiberger in their book, *Fuzzy Logic* write: "The Jains built a formal logic in which existence and nonexistence inhere in everything. Every statement is partly true and partly false. There is no certainty, at least none we can know."

Around 500 B.C. lived the philosopher Sakyamuni, better known as the Buddha. The philosophy of the Buddha closely resembled that of the Jains. The Buddha was one of the first philosophers to reject the black and white view of reality in favor of shades of gray. He saw the world filled with contradictions — with things being both **A** and, at the same time, *not* **A**.

Daoism originated from the work of Lao Zi (the "Old Master"). It emphasizes the wisdom of seeing the contradictory in the whole. Each opposite endpoint on a continuum requires the other endpoint. There is even a kind of imperfection to perfection. In short, wisdom lies in paradox, and the superior person accepts apparent contradictions.

118    *Shades of Reality*

Partial contradiction is expressed by the Chinese concept of *yin* and *yang*. Its most famous emblem, the *tai ji tu*, is shown in Figure 7.1. It is a circle divided into two equal areas of black and white with each part containing a circle of the opposite color. The small circles represent the Daoist idea that once anything reaches its extreme limit, it begins to create its opposite.

Figure 7.1

Buddhism has had a strong impact on Japanese culture. With this kind of upbringing, the Japanese have accepted vagueness as a way of life. As McNeill and Freiberger write:

> Their language reflects it. In fact, it is not inherently vaguer than any other tongue, but the Japanese deploy it in an extraordinary way. . . . For instance, the Japanese rely heavily on context. They omit the subject and object of a sentence wherever possible. The same noun can be either singular or plural, like *you* in English, and verbs provide no clue to their number. Verbs also lack the fairly precise indications of time found in Western languages.

It is therefore not surprising that the Japanese have come to accept fuzzy logic much more readily than have Americans. Japan has thousands of fuzzy specialists, most of them working on developing special-purpose industrial applications.

## The Philosophy of Science

Unlike the philosophies of the East, Western science is based on a dogma of exactness and precision. There is no room for vagueness and ambiguity. Western scientists demand that theories and hypotheses be clearly and unambiguously defined. For example Western science would say that the gravitational force decreases inversely with the square of the distance between two objects. Fuzzy science might simply say that objects that are far apart experience less force of gravity between them than objects that are close together, without precisely indicating what the terms "close" and "far" mean.

This kind of scientific laxness has prompted much criticism of fuzzy logic, particularly when it was first introduced. In the words of Rudolf Kalman (1972), the inventor of the Kalman filter: "'Fuzzification' is a kind of scientific permissiveness; it tends to result in socially appealing slogans unaccompanied by the discipline of hard scientific work and patient observation. I must confess that I cannot conceive of 'fuzzification' as a viable alternative for the scientific method."

In 1975 the mathematician William Kahan stated: "What we need is more logical thinking, not less. The danger of fuzzy theory is that it will encourage the sort of imprecise thinking that has brought us into so much trouble."

A requirement of any scientific theory is not only that it can be *verified* by experiment, but that it can also be potentially *disproved* by experiment. If an experiment produces a result that contradicts the theory, then some kind of reformulation of the theory is required. As Kahan points out:

> But with fuzzy sets, the existence of contradictory sets doesn't cause things to malfunction. Contradictory information doesn't lead to a clash. You just keep computing. . . . Logic isn't following the rules of Aristotle blindly. It takes the kind of pain known to the runner. He knows he is

## Shades of Reality

doing something. When you are thinking about something hard, you'll feel a similar sort of pain. Fuzzy logic is marvelous. It insulates you from pain. It is the cocaine of science.

But the term "fuzzy" has two slightly different meanings. In addition to meaning "vague," fuzzy also means "shades of gray" (or having a range of values). And science certainly accepts *that* concept. Otherwise, the very idea of *measurement* would be meaningless.

### Western Philosophy

As we have already indicated, much of western philosophy is based on the teachings of Aristotle and his black and white views of reality. Aristotle's philosophy could not accept apparent contradictions or vagueness. Something was either **A**, or else it *wasn't* **A**. (Because no middle ground was admissible, this concept is sometimes referred to as the *law of excluded middle*.) Something was either black, or else it was white. A person was either tall, or else they weren't.

In view of the Western world's propensity to shun fuzziness and vagueness, it is somewhat surprising that fast-food restaurants in this country generally offer soft drinks in "fuzzy sizes" (e.g., "small," "medium," and "large") instead of specifying the amount in precise numerical terms (like ounces). But when it comes to *paying* for those drinks, there is absolutely *no* ambiguity in the *price*. It's specified right down to the exact penny!

It is fashionable to use clichés in our everyday speech. One popular cliché you sometimes hear is the phrase, "There are no absolutes, only shades of gray." These words are sometimes uttered in quasi-intellectual discussion groups when one of the speakers in the group begins expounding an extreme point of view. But then that same person will often contradict that very concept later by saying to somebody, "You don't *know* what

*Fuzzy Logic in the Real World*     121

you're talking about" (as if he has changed his mind about there being only shades of gray and now believes that "knowing" is an all-or-nothing state in which a person either totally *does* know what he is talking about, or else he totally *doesn't*!).

Clearly, the concept of shades of gray is not a difficult one. Even a baby can distinguish a dark gray toy from a light gray one. We look at a "black and white" photograph and see shades of gray virtually everywhere. We all can recognize gray as a color, and we are certainly intelligent enough to know how to extrapolate the shades-of-gray concept to non-color applications. So why do Americans have such a difficult time with fuzzy logic?

Most of the reason has to do with how we are brought up. From the time we were little children we were told to ignore the grays and to treat reality as if it had sharply defined boundary lines, just like the black and white line drawings in our coloring books. And when we filled in those coloring book pictures with our crayons, we always used one solid color for each object, and we were very careful to never color past the black boundary lines.

The athletic games we played also incorporated simple boundary lines: a baseball was hit either fair, or else it was foul. A football player either stepped out-of-bounds, or else he didn't. A basketball player either scored a basket, or else he didn't. Except in horseshoes, there were no *partial* points for being *close*. Everything was either all, or nothing.

With this kind of lifelong indoctrination it's not too surprising that we would grow up to view reality itself as nothing more than a black and white game: A person is either an adult or else is a minor, a person has either committed a crime, or else he hasn't. A fetus is either a human being, or else it isn't.

The Aristotelian mentality is a difficult one to discard, and I too have trouble with it occasionally. Several years ago while on a driving trip through a remote part of Alaska, my motor home's engine started to overheat. Whenever the little red indicator light

## 122    *Shades of Reality*

on my dashboard came on, I would become very worried. But after a few minutes it would go off, and I would breathe a sigh of relief now that everything was OK again!

Actually, most of us already accept the fundamental ideas of fuzzy logic, and we don't even realize it! For example are you aware that your automobile has many fuzzy devices on it? One of them is a gadget for precisely adjusting the direction of the vehicle's velocity vector. The device is called the *steering wheel*! It lets you choose the amount of "sharpness" of a turn. If the steering wheel had been designed as a non-fuzzy device (such as a pair of steering push-buttons, one for turning left and one for turning right) then there would have been no shades of gray to turning — the wheels of the car would have always turned either all the way to the left or else all the way to the right! (Remember, the term "fuzzy" simply means allowing for intermediate values between two extreme limits.)

Other fuzzy devices on your car include the gas pedal (to provide a range of accelerations), the brake pedal (to provide a range of decelerations), the volume control on the radio (to provide a range of loudness), and even the clock (to indicate more than just "daytime" or "nighttime")!

And when you pull into a gas station, you don't pay one fixed "fill-up fee" regardless of how much gas you take. You pay only for what you get. A non-fuzzy approach might have been to have you pay zero dollars if you take *less* than 1 gallon, and $20 if you take *more* than 1 gallon. In other words you would either pay all (of the $20), or nothing.

You might want to say that these examples represent nothing but plain old common sense. You've got it! Fuzzy logic is merely the process of looking at reality *realistically*! Reality isn't a made-up game like football or baseball where *we* invent the rules. Reality has its *own* rules.

And even when we play games where we *do* invent the rules, there is no need to always insist that the outcomes of those

*Fuzzy Logic in the Real World*     123

games always be of an Aristotelian nature. For example let's once again consider the game of Pitching Pennies, which we discussed in Chapter Three.

**Pitching Pennies**

Suppose you and I have agreed to play Pitching Pennies. Each of us will take turns tossing our pennies into the circle. When it's your turn to do the tossing, you will get to keep only those pennies that end up inside the circle, and I will get all the pennies that land outside the circle, and similarly for you when it's *my* turn to do the tossing.

Let's suppose that you have just finished tossing eight pennies and they ended up as shown in Figure 7.2.

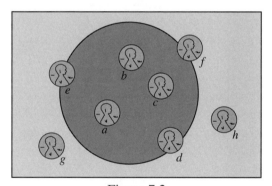

Figure 7.2

Clearly pennies **a**, **b**, and **c** would belong to you, and pennies **g** and **h** would belong to me. But what about the pennies that landed "on the line"? Who would get pennies **d**, **e**, and **f** (the ones that landed partly inside the circle and partly outside)?

The "American" way (with its Aristotelian "you-gotta-draw-the-line-somewhere" mentality) of solving the problem would be to "round off" the results by declaring a penny to be

## 124    *Shades of Reality*

inside the circle if most of it is inside the circle (and to declare it as being outside the circle if most of it is outside). Therefore, penny **d** would belong to you, and penny **f** would belong to me. And if we were to continue our game for a long time, the results of such a "rounding-off" approach would kind of "average out" into a wash. In the long run the number of "on the line" pennies that land more than half way *inside* the circle would about equal the number of pennies that land more than half way *outside*.

But who would get penny **e**, the one that landed exactly halfway in, and halfway out? Of course it's easy to simply dismiss the problem. After all, it's only a penny. So maybe you might decide to be magnanimous and concede the coin to me. And the next time it happens I might concede the penny to you.

But suppose that, instead of pennies, we were to use something substantially more valuable, such as silver dollars or gold coins. And instead of playing the game hundreds of times (where statistics can "average out" the results), let's play the game only *once*.

We each toss our one and only silver dollar into the circle. Mine lands completely inside the circle, and yours lands on the line — 1/4 inside the circle, and 3/4 outside. What is the fairest and most realistic way to determine the winner of the money?

Since *my* toss landed completely inside the circle, I am clearly entitled to keep my silver dollar. But some parts of *your* dollar landed inside the circle, and some parts landed outside. Since we agreed that you would be entitled to keep whatever money you tossed that landed *inside* the circle, it wouldn't be fair for me to take *all* of your dollar just because *most* of it landed outside the circle. You have a legitimate claim to all of the silver atoms that *did* make it into the circle. Therefore the fairest solution to the problem would be for you to keep your silver dollar and to pay me 75 cents (since, in reality, I only have a 75 percent claim on your coin).

By using this kind of "shades of gray" approach for deter-

*Fuzzy Logic in the Real World*    125

mining the winner, the reality of *the actual outcome of each coin-toss is preserved*. There is no need to "round off" this reality to some Aristotelian *non*-reality by always declaring only one person or the other to be the *total* winner. Both players win (but to different degrees) when the coin lands on the line.

This example illustrates an important feature of fuzzy logic: **Fuzzy solutions to problems can be reality-preserving**. (We will utilize this feature more fully in Chapter Nine when we discuss the concept of Realistic laws.)

### Statistical Fuzziness

But what about those instances in which there simply *aren't* any shades of gray available? What do you do when the only choices available are two opposite *extremes*? What do you do when you simply "*gotta* draw the line" and make a choice between one of those extremes or the other?

For example consider a gun. There aren't too many shades of gray about shooting — either the bullet gets fired, or it doesn't. (Pulling the trigger only halfway doesn't make the bullet come out only half as fast!) It's an *all-or-nothing* result.

Now, imagine that you are standing in an open clearing in the jungle. Off in the distance is a ferocious tiger. As he slowly approaches, you raise your rifle to the ready position. You don't really want to shoot the poor beast unless you absolutely have to. After all, maybe he's only curious about you. Maybe he'll turn around and go away if you just don't antagonize him. But still, he keeps coming closer . . . and closer . . . .

How close should you let him come before you decide that you have to pull the trigger? *At what distance do you "draw the line" between shooting him and not shooting him?*

While this represents a valid example of sometimes having to "draw the line somewhere," it also illustrates another form of fuzziness, which I call *statistical* fuzziness.

## 126    *Shades of Reality*

Imagine that the above tiger encounter was not just a one-time event, but that it happened on hundreds of different occasions under virtually the same circumstances. Let's say that as long as each tiger remained at least 20 feet away, you felt reasonably "safe" and you always refrained from pulling the trigger. On the other hand, no tiger ever got closer than 10 feet from you without him having to pay the supreme penalty. (Assume all shots were fatal.) At intermediate distances (such as 13 or 14 feet), some of the tigers were allowed to survive, while others were shot as far away as 17 or 18 feet.

Therefore, even though each individual tiger was shot at a different "crisp" distance (at which you "drew the line" for that particular encounter), the *entire* set of "don't-pull-the-trigger" distances that resulted from *all* of the encounters was a *fuzzy* set (a "statistically" fuzzy set). A given fixed distance, such as 15 feet, was both a member of that set and also a member of the *complement* set. (But for any *particular* encounter, its membership value in either the "pull-the-trigger" set or its complement was always crisp — i.e., either 0 percent, or 100 percent). There was no single exact distance at which you *always* "drew the line" between pulling the trigger and *not* pulling the trigger. Instead, the collective result was simply: the closer that each tiger came, the *more likely* it was that he would get shot.

This concept of statistical fuzziness suggests at least one possible approach for introducing shades of gray into matters that seem to require the drawing of a black and white boundary line somewhere. Let's consider the question of how a person's age should be used to determine his or her voting rights.

Just as in our example of shooting the tigers, we might view the matter of determining voting rights as having to decide at what age we should "pull the trigger" in allowing each person to vote. Instead of merely "drawing the line" at 18 years of age (or *any* age), we *could* allow a certain percentage of 17-year-olds to vote. And we could allow an even *smaller* percentage of 16-year-

*Fuzzy Logic in the Real World* 127

olds to vote, and so on.

Before every election each teenage citizen in the country could be allowed to apply for the right to vote. (The process might be handled in a manner similar to a lottery.) The older the person is, the better his chances would be of "winning" one of those voting rights. By the time he reached 21 years of age (or whatever), his "chance" of being allowed to vote would finally reach 100 percent (i.e., he would *always* be allowed to vote). This approach would eliminate the necessity of having to "draw the line" at an arbitrary (and therefore meaningless) minimum age limit. (In Chapter Nine we will see an even *better* way of handling this voting rights issue.)

Statistical fuzziness does not necessarily require "randomness." For example statistical fuzziness is also the basis for the process known as "halftone printing." (In computer graphics a similar technique is called "dithering.") If you look at a "black and white" photograph in a newspaper and examine it carefully with a magnifying glass, you will see that the gray portions of the image are *not* printed with gray ink. Instead, gray is produced by printing tiny black dots on a white background. Any microscopic point on the paper therefore contains either black ink or no ink at all, but the resulting *macroscopic* visual effect is a shade of *gray* for that particular region. The higher the ratio of black dots to white, the darker the apparent shade of gray. In this way a printed photograph can be displayed without the printer having to "draw the line" in terms of which regions of the image should be printed as totally black, and which regions should be printed as totally white. Because of statistical fuzziness the entire image can be presented *realistically*, i.e., in *shades of gray!*

## Kicking the Aristotelian Habit

If you really want to kick the Aristotelian habit, your thinking is going to have to undergo a complete overhaul. You will

128    *Shades of Reality*

need to shift paradigms, and that's not going to be an easy thing to do. It's not sufficient to merely *acknowledge* the existence of fuzzy reality with its shades of gray. You are going to have to make a conscious effort to *think* in fuzzy terms as well. Just as in the case of E-Prime (see "Introduction to Reality" at the beginning of this book) you might start out by becoming aware of the terms that you use in everyday speech. Try to keep yourself from using phrases that contain all-or-nothing implications such as:

> "George is a good person."
> "I had no idea that . . ."
> "At some point in time . . ."
> "I would be perfectly happy to . . ."
> "You are wrong about . . ."
> "Everybody is talking about . . ."
>               etc.

Instead, train yourself to use more *correct* phrases like:

> "George is a person with a high
>      *degree of goodness.*"
> "I had no more than a very *low*
>      *degree of awareness* that . . ."
> "During some interval of time . . ."
> "It would give me a *high degree*
>      *of happiness* to . . ."
> "You have no more than a *low degree*
>      *of correctness* about . . ."
> "*A high percentage of the population*
>      is talking about . . ."
>               etc.

These new phrases will sound awkward and unnatural at first, but they will help drive home the fuzzy principle (that everything is a matter of degree).

*Fuzzy Logic in the Real World*     129

And above all, try to avoid using the phrase:

"Well, you gotta draw the line somewhere."

While there *are* times when there is no other alternative but to "draw the line," most Americans are far too quick to automatically adopt such a solution as being the *only* possibility, and never even bother to *look* for other plausible approaches. However (as we will see in the remainder of this book), most societal issues can be resolved without having to resort to Aristotelian "line drawing."

# Chapter Eight

# The Laws of the Land

The American legal system is generally acknowledged (at least by Americans) as being one of the best in the world. All of the "bad guys" go to jail, and all of the "good guys" go free, right? In a court of law *everybody* is always treated equally, right? There is *no possible way* the system could be made better, right?

Imagine that you have just been appointed to become the king (or the queen) of a brand new country and that you, as the supreme authority, are to define the legal system that will henceforth become the "Laws of the Land." What would you do? (No, you're not allowed to *abdicate*!) Would you become a dictator? Would you establish an aristocracy that granted special privileges and favors to certain members of society? Would you implement an American-type of legal system?

Let's suppose that you are noble and altruistic enough to resist selfish temptations of greed, and that your newly acquired absolute power and supreme authority don't simply go to your head. Let's suppose that you sincerely want to try to create the best possible legal system that you can imagine — one that was

*The Law of the Land*    131

both just and fair for everybody in the kingdom. What would *you* do?

**If *I* Were King**

If *I* were king, I would solve the problem by appointing a Royal Legislation Committee to make and enforce the laws *for* me! This may sound like a "cop-out" (no pun intended), but it's really not. Before I would turn my committee loose, I would *demand* that each person on the committee adhere to a simple **Prime Directive of Equality**. At first I wouldn't care what *specific* laws they would legislate or how they would choose to enforce them. But I would make it abundantly clear that *every* law and its enforcement *must* be implemented in accordance with my Prime Directive:

### Prime Directive of Equality

**If any two citizens of the kingdom separately commit almost identical actions under almost identical circumstances, then the legal consequences of each of those two separate actions *must* be almost identical as well.**

Of course in real life no two separate actions are ever *exactly* identical, nor do they ever occur under *exactly* the same circumstances. But the Prime Directive of Equality says that I would not allow *grossly different* legal consequences to result from two *nearly identical* cases. The more similar any two cases would be to each other, the more similar I would require the legal outcomes of those cases to be.

Any law or courtroom verdict that did not conform to the Prime Directive of Equality would be immediately rejected. Every law that survived would therefore be fair and just for

132    *Shades of Reality*

everybody. The Prime Directive of Equality would be the foundation of the entire legal system in my kingdom.

I wish that the Prime Directive of Equality could have been the foundation of the legal system in the United States, but unfortunately it's *not*! Furthermore, the laws in the United States don't even *pretend* to conform to this concept, even in *principle*! In fact,

**The entire legal system of the United States openly and publicly rejects the Prime Directive of Equality!**

I would suspect that this fact comes as a bit of a surprise to you. Perhaps you're thinking to yourself: "What kind of a nonsense statement is *that* to make? How dare you say that the United States rejects the idea of equality! Why, this country was *founded* on the principles of freedom and equality for everyone. It says so right in The Declaration of Independence: 'We hold these truths to be self-evident that all men are created equal.' So how dare you make such an absurd statement about our legal system not believing in equality!"

And yet, my statement remains *true*. (But before I explain what I mean, you might want to close the book for a few minutes and think about it. See if you can figure out for yourself just what it is that I'm getting at.)

### The American Legal System

Of course *corruption* can exist in any government, even in America. Some members of the police force and certain public officials might be "paid off" in exchange for favors. The results could certainly lead to violations of the Prime Directive of Equality. *But that's not what I'm referring to in my previous statement.*

Surely, being able to afford a good attorney can help get a person acquitted, as we all saw in the O. J. Simpson criminal

*The Law of the Land*     133

trial. Without access to such lawyers a similar defendant under exactly the same circumstances might have been convicted. *But that's not what I'm referring to either.*

Perhaps you think I'm referring to racial issues in which a white person on trial for a crime might get treated differently than a non-white. Nope, even *that* is not what I'm getting at.

How about witnesses who lie on the witness stand? Or how about cases in which it simply comes down to *your* word vs. somebody *else's* word? Or how about when a witness simply makes a mistake when testifying? Is that what you think I'm referring to? The answers to each of those questions are: no, no, and no, respectively.

What I'm referring to are not contrived, covert, or "once in a blue moon" types of examples. Nor are they the result of human frailties such as greed, prejudice, dishonesty, or even simple judgment errors. The kinds of things I'm talking about happen literally *millions* of times each day and in thousands of different ways. And they all happen with your complete cognizance and full approval!

Give up? Then let me give you just a very few examples. After you see the first one or two, you will surely be able to come up with hundreds of examples of your own.

### Voting

The United States divides its citizens into two groups (or pseudocategories): those who are 18 years of age or older, and those who are less than 18 years of age. Members of the former group are allowed full and complete voting privileges. Members of the latter group are not allowed to vote at all.

Now consider two typical teenagers, virtually identical in every respect — they each have similar levels of intelligence, similar attitudes and social values, and similar ages. However, one of the teenagers just celebrated his eighteenth birthday *yesterday*, while the other teenager will be celebrating his eighteenth

134 *Shades of Reality*

birthday *tomorrow*. Today is election day. Each of the boys walks into the polling place. The two boys are virtually identical in age. In fact you would be hard pressed to determine which boy is older simply by looking at them or by talking to them. But as each one tries to step into a voting booth, one is allowed to proceed while the other one is denied access — a clear violation of the Prime Directive of Equality!

In my kingdom no such arbitrary discrimination would be tolerated. If *one* of two virtually identical teenagers is granted a right to vote, then the *other* teenager would *also* have to be granted a similar voting right. *But not so in America*! (In the next chapter I will present the *Realistic* solution to the voting issue, a solution that *doesn't* violate the Prime Directive of Equality and, at the same time, still limits the voting rights of "minors.")

## Speeding

Imagine two virtually identical automobiles being driven by two virtually identical drivers on a road where the speed limit is 65 mph. One driver is traveling at 65 mph and the other driver is traveling at 67 mph. A policeman observes both drivers moving along the highway. The latter driver receives a speeding ticket, while the former driver proceeds unhindered — another flagrant violation of the Prime Directive of Equality. (If 65 mph is to be considered as a "safe and acceptable" speed, then 67 mph cannot be regarded as being *substantially* less "safe and acceptable." Conversely, if 67 mph *is* "unsafe and unacceptable," then so too must 65 mph be just about as "unsafe and unacceptable" — because the two speeds are virtually the same.)

## Driving While Intoxicated

In California it is illegal for any person with a blood alcohol content of 0.08 or higher to operate a motor vehicle.

*The Law of the Land*     135

Consider two virtually identical automobiles being operated by two virtually identical drivers under virtually identical levels of intoxication. Policemen stop each vehicle and test the drivers for sobriety. One of the drivers is found to have an intoxication level of 0.079 while the other driver is measured at 0.081. One of the drivers is arrested for driving while intoxicated, while the other driver is set free — another violation of the Prime Directive of Equality. (If 0.081 represents "intoxicated" then 0.079 is just as "intoxicated" for all practical purposes. By the same token, if 0.079 is to be considered as *not* being intoxicated, then how can 0.081 be regarded as representing a *substantially different* level of sobriety?)

### Purchasing of Tobacco Products

It is illegal for any person under 18 years of age to purchase tobacco products, such as cigarettes.

Again, consider two teenagers of virtually identical age — except that one celebrated his 18th birthday yesterday, while the other will be celebrating his 18th birthday tomorrow. The former is allowed to purchase cigarettes, while the latter is prohibited.

I could continue on and discuss the minimum legal drinking age, and the laws that prohibit parking too close to a fire hydrant, and the laws that establish the minimum size fish that fishermen are allowed to catch, etc., etc., but I think you've gotten the idea by now. All of these laws involve partitioning a continuum into two parts by drawing some completely arbitrary boundary line, and then equifying one of the two parts to "*legal*" and equifying the other part to "*illegal*." (If your only response to this is: "Well, we gotta draw the line *somewhere*," then you had better go back and carefully reread Part One of this book.)

136   *Shades of Reality*

**The "Game" of Law**

Legislators and other members of the legal profession view reality as little more than a game of make-believe. The game is played on a playing field consisting of only black and white areas separated by perfectly straight horizontal and vertical boundary lines. The white areas represent "legal" and the black areas represent "illegal." The shades of reality don't exist for legal professionals. Their minds see only black or white — legal or illegal — guilty or not guilty.

There are no gently rolling hills and valleys on the landscape of law. There are only sheer cliffs and flat lands in this fantasy world. A "mountain" is nothing more than a cube (with perfectly vertical sides and a flat top) resting on a perfectly flat plane.

There is no twilight in this Aristotelian land — at any point in time it's either bright daylight outside, or else it's pitch dark.

Like a bit inside of a computer, legal professionals can interpret only ones and zeros. If such "bit-brained" individuals were to look at the picture shown in Figure 8.1 they would not

Figure 8.1

see any regions of smooth transition between black and white. They would not notice the areas containing delicate fine structure and subtle shades of gray. Instead, they would see only Figure 8.2. *This*, to them, is reality:

Figure 8.2

I can hear them complaining: "Objection, Your Honor! The party of the first part (yours truly) is *completely wrong*! The law *does* allow for grayness. A judge has the right to take into account 'extenuating circumstances,' and, in so doing, he may reduce the sentence to any level that he deems appropriate."

"Objection overruled!" is my reply. Because "penalty" and "verdict" are two completely separate issues. Even if the *penalty* is reduced, the *verdict* still remains at *100 percent guilty*. The only way to reduce the *verdict* would be to either change it all the way down to 0 percent guilty (i.e., not guilty), or else declare the defendant guilty of a *lesser* crime (but still *100 percent guilty* of that lesser crime).

Our legal system acknowledges only all-or-nothing guilt. This means that if you perform some action (for example, speeding), and if that action is just barely "bad enough," then you are

138     *Shades of Reality*

declared to be *guilty* of that action — totally and completely 100 percent guilty. However, if somebody performs almost the same action, but *just misses* being "bad enough," then they are declared to be *not* guilty — totally and completely 100 percent not guilty.

I rest my case!

## Presumption of Guilt

In some countries, a person accused of a crime is presumed to be totally guilty of that crime until proven otherwise. It then becomes the burden of the accused person to clear himself. In our country, a person accused of a crime is presumed to be totally *not* guilty. It then becomes the burden of the *victim(s)* of the crime to prove otherwise.

Our legal system seems to bend over backwards to protect the rights of criminals. Even when they are *convicted* of a crime, criminals are often back out on the streets again after a short time, either on parole or because of reduced sentences. And when they commit a crime that has not yet come to trial, we, in effect, congratulate them for not yet having done anything wrong!

Of course the reason for our presumption of non-guilt stems from the possibility that the accused person might, in actuality, *be* totally not guilty (even though *total* non-guilt seldom exists in the real world), and therefore they should not have to wrongfully suffer because of the crime. But what about the *victim(s)* of the crime? What is the "possibility" that *they* "might" have wrongfully suffered because of the crime? Should we "presume" that a person who has been murdered *isn't really dead* until his murderer is actually convicted? Our laws protect the rights of criminals, but nothing retroactively protects the "rights" of those criminals' *victims.*

A totally fair legal system would not make any extreme presumptions of guilt either one way or the other. Instead, it would

*The Law of the Land*     139

adopt a "wait and see" attitude — a person accused of a crime would simply be "suspect" of the crime. But if for some reason a presumption regarding his guilt were to be needed, he would be presumed to be only 1/2 guilty. (Actually, such a state of partial guilt already *does* exist in our present legal system. When a person accused of a major crime is awaiting trial, that person is kept in *jail* — hardly the way to treat someone who is allegedly being presumed *not* guilty of the crime!)

**Partial Guilt**

It's a cool autumn afternoon in busy downtown Chicago. An elderly gentleman with gray hair and glasses sits quietly on a nearby park bench reading a newspaper while passersby walk to-and-fro tending to other matters, important and mundane. Suddenly, from out of the bushes steps a dark figure holding a dagger. "Look out"! screams a nearby woman. "He's got a knife"! The dark figure glares silently at the woman for a moment. "He can't hear you, bitch! He's deaf." Before the elderly gentleman can even look up from his newspaper, the knife plunges into his back, and he slumps to the ground. The assailant runs off through the crowded streets and disappears. The elderly gentleman is rushed to a nearby hospital where he later dies. A suspect is eventually found who matches the description of the killer, and the suspect is brought to trial.

The above scenario represents the kind of incident for which a fairly "crisp" all-or-nothing guilt can probably be assigned. The murder was committed by a single assailant. Therefore, the suspect in custody either *is* the killer, or else he *isn't*. And it now becomes the task of the court to try and determine which of these two alternatives is the truth. The case is therefore an easy, "Perry Mason" type of case. By "easy," I mean that if all of the facts in the case were known, the court would be able to

140     *Shades of Reality*

say with a high degree of accuracy that the suspect is either 100 percent guilty, or 100 percent not guilty — the kind of crisp verdict that conforms well with the American public's stereotype of criminal guilt.

But what if an *accomplice* had been involved? Should the woman who screamed be considered an accomplice simply because she saw the murder about to happen and had several seconds in which she might have tried to intervene, but chose not to risk her own life by doing anything more to stop the murder than merely screaming? How about all of the *other* bystanders? Might one of *them* have been able to prevent the murder from happening?

Try to imagine an infinite *continuum* of slightly different murder scenarios, each filled with different bystanders. Imagine that, in each scenario, the bystanders have different degrees of advance knowledge of the murder (ranging continuously from no knowledge at all . . . to a slight hunch . . . to complete knowledge). Further imagine that each bystander has a different degree of hatred for the old man ranging continuously from 0 percent (total indifference) to 100 percent (wanting to see him dead). And finally, imagine that each of the bystanders has a different degree of either direct or potential involvement in the incident, ranging continuously from 0 percent (didn't even see the murder happen) to 100 percent (standing right next to the assailant, ready to hand the knife back to him if he should accidentally drop it!)

Now the matter is not so easy and clear-cut. Even if *all* of the facts in the case were to become known — even if *God* were able to come down and testify as to what each person's exact thoughts were — how would you decide where (in the three-dimensional continuum of *knowledge, hatred*, and *involvement*) to arbitrarily draw the "line" (or, more properly, the "surface") separating "accomplice" from "non-accomplice"? Where in this "twilight" area, which separates guilt from non-guilt, would you draw the line between "day" and "night"? Which of the infinite

*The Law of the Land* 141

continuum of bystanders *should* be required to go to prison, and which ones *shouldn't*?

To *some* degree, *all* of the infinite number of hypothetical bystanders would be guilty of being accomplices. But the degrees of guilt would range anywhere from 0 percent (totally *not* an accomplice) all the way up to 100 percent (a *full* accomplice). And so each person would *not* simply either "be" an accomplice or "not" be one. Instead each bystander would be *partially* guilty of being an accomplice to whatever extent that he or she actually *was* an accomplice.


As another example of the concept of partial guilt, consider the crime of battery. How hard must a person hit someone in order for the hitter to be "guilty" of battery?

Let's suppose you are walking down the sidewalk and another person passing by accidentally brushes lightly against the sleeve of your shirt. Is that person guilty of battery? Of course not. Let's suppose the next person who passes by also brushes lightly against your sleeve, only this time the contact is ever so slightly greater than in the previous brush. Is this second person guilty of battery? Of course not.

But now let's suppose that you go through the whole day experiencing thousands of such encounters, with each new "brush" occurring with just a *tiny* bit more contact and enthusiasm than the one just before it. By the end of the day the encounters will have gotten to be so violent that the persons hitting you will clearly be "guilty" of battery. But there would have been no specific point at which the guilts suddenly "switched on." Just as in the sorites paradox of trying to find the point at which a "heap" of sand becomes a "non-heap," you would not be able to point to any two consecutive encounters, one of which was clearly *not* a case of battery, while the second of which clearly *was* a case of battery. Instead, each subsequent person who

## 142   *Shades of Reality*

bumped you would have simply been a little bit "more guilty" of battery than was his predecessor.

However, the reality of partial guilt (or equivalently, the *partial existence* of guilt) doesn't fit into the American legal system's "fantasy" of a black and white world — an Aristotelian game of *total* guilt vs. total *non*-guilt. And whenever reality conflicts with fantasy, something's got to give. And so it's *reality* that gets rejected!

# Chapter Nine

# Realistic Law

Many public parks have signs at their entrances proclaiming the times during which the park is open. Sometimes the hours of operation are explicitly stated in terms of clock times, such as:

Lincoln State Park Hours: 8 AM to 10 PM, Everyday

But some parks have less precise signs proclaiming their hours of operation:

Jackson City Park: Open Only During Daylight Hours

Either way, the signs indicate that there are times during which you are not supposed to be inside the park.

Now let's imagine that every park decides to incorporate a very strict rule: *Any unauthorized person found inside the park after hours will be fined $100*. Therefore, if a person were to be caught inside Lincoln Park after 10 PM or before 8 AM the next day, they would clearly be subject to a $100 fine. But what about Jackson Park? At what specific times does daylight begin and end?

The "American way" of dealing with this kind of problem would be to simply go and change the park sign so that it pre-

143

sented explicit *clock* times! Of course the new sign would no longer reflect the original intent — that the park is supposed to remain open during all daylight hours (since sunset and the ensuing darkness occurs at a different time each day). But then "you gotta draw the line *somewhere*," right?

**Park Trespassing — the Realistic Solution**

I would like to propose an even simpler approach to solving this problem — an approach that doesn't require the changing of any signs, and which doesn't require the "gotta drawing" of any lines.

We know that at any instant in time the question, "Is it dark yet?" has an answer that is both "yes" to some degree and "no" to some degree. Or equivalently, the question, "To what degree is it dark?" has an answer that lies somewhere between 0 percent and 100 percent. The numerical value of this degree of darkness could be determined from a standard lookup table, which would express the degree of darkness as a function of time for each day of the year.

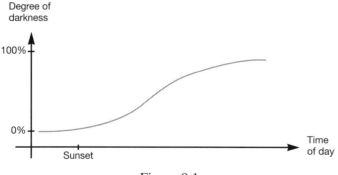

Figure 9.1

Or each ranger could simply be equipped with an ordinary light meter for measuring the level of darkness at any time.

Therefore, the degree to which a person would be guilty of trespassing could simply be determined by the current degree of darkness, i.e., the degree of guilt at any particular point in time could simply be equal to that time's membership value in the fuzzy set called "dark." For example if it's 25 percent of the way to becoming totally dark, then a person caught inside Jackson Park might be 25 percent guilty of trespassing, and he might therefore be fined 25 percent of the total fine (i.e., $25.)*

I refer to this kind of approach to legal issues as *Realistic* law, because it is based on the shades of gray of *reality* (instead of the blacks and whites of some *mind game*). Rather than trying to equify partial guilt into pseudocategories of "100 percent guilt" and "100 percent non-guilt" Realistic Law simply acknowledges the truth — a person is only as guilty as he really *is*. There is no need to *round off* this true level of guilt to the nearest "totally guilty" or "totally *not* guilty."

But there is an even more important feature of this approach:

### Realistic Laws never violate
### the Prime Directive of Equality.

For example in Jackson Park there is no point at which the guilt and the corresponding fine suddenly get "turned on." Instead they both increase smoothly from 0 percent to 100 percent since they are both tied to the smoothly changing level of darkness. Therefore, two *nearly identical* trespassers will always be *nearly identically* guilty, and they will always pay *nearly identi-*

---

\* As a practical matter, the degree of guilt of trespassing would *not* necessarily have to be *linearly proportional* to the current level of darkness. Instead the guilt curve could still remain low even for moderate levels of darkness, and only begin to rise substantially (but in a continuous manner) as it becomes significantly dark. This would allow visitors to be inside the park on dark cloudy days and not have them be significantly guilty of trespassing.

146     *Shades of Reality*

*cal* fines (in accordance with the Prime Directive of Equality). Contrast this with the *non*-Realistic law governing trespassers in Lincoln Park. A person caught in the park at 9:59 PM is *not guilty* of trespassing. But two minutes later, if another person is caught in the park, he is guilty of trespassing and must pay the $100 fine, clearly a violation of the Prime Directive of Equality.

Perhaps you are thinking that the Prime Directive of Equality could have been satisfied by simply offering a "grace period" to trespassers — if someone is just a little late in leaving Lincoln Park, then merely have the park ranger "look the other way" and let him go. That way a person leaving at 10:01 or 10:02 would still be treated the same as a person leaving at 9:59. But a moment's reflection reveals that implementing a grace period resolves absolutely *nothing*. For then you must still face the problem of deciding where to "draw the line" between grace period (when *no* fine gets issued), and *non*-grace period (when a fine *does* get issued). Implementing a grace period does nothing more than merely shift the park's closing hour to a later time. And you are then still left with the problem of satisfying the Prime Directive at this *new* later time.

Imagine that you are the ranger in charge, and let's suppose that there are several hundred visitors still inside the park. As dusk approaches, they all start to file out slowly, one by one, at about 5 or 10 second intervals. After which person should the grace period suddenly end? And after you've established that arbitrary cutoff point, how would you handle the valid objection from the person in line who says: "But you let the guy in *front* of me go out without fining *him* anything. So why should *I* have to pay a fine?" You would be stuck with a sorites problem. (You'd still be stuck with the same sorites problem in principle, even if you *didn't* offer a grace period.)

Realistic law is a subset of a more general concept that might be referred to as *fuzzy* (or multivalent) law. For example, a

*Realistic Law* 147

park trespasser might have had his level of guilt decided by a *random number generator* instead of by the level of darkness. While this, too, would have been fuzzy (in the sense that it would have produced shades of gray between "guilty" and "not guilty"), it would not have been a *realistic* solution. Realistic law is therefore based on a particular *type* of fuzziness known as *reality*. And because Realistic laws are consistent with reality, Realistic laws are *more correct* (see Chapter Zero) than non-Realistic laws.

Recall the Smoothness Principle of reality (see Chapter One), which states that everything in physical reality occurs smoothly. The Prime Directive of Equality therefore imposes a smoothness requirement to law. One can state a corresponding "Smoothness Principle" for Realistic law:

***Everything in Realistic law occurs smoothly.***

Realistic laws do not have sharp cutoff points defined by arbitrary black and white boundary lines. "Legal" gently blends into "illegal," just as "day" gently blends into "night."

## Voting

Voting is the democratic process in which we all get to express our choices about political issues and candidates. It is a process that requires both maturity and a fundamental understanding of the issues on the ballot. But how do we determine "maturity"? How can we measure "understanding"? Should we allow absolutely everyone to vote, or do we "gotta draw the line somewhere"?

Before a person is allowed to drive an automobile, he must first pass a series of tests to prove his proficiency and knowledge of the rules of the road. Perhaps it would be a good idea to require potential voters to pass a similar kind of proficiency test to prove that they can at least understand the issues on the ballot. Otherwise, without the requirement of such an understanding, we might just as well let *little children* have full voting rights too!

But, once again, such is not the "American way." To be eligible to vote, the only requirement is that you be a warm-bodied citizen older than some completely arbitrary cutoff age (usually 18). You are then equified into being "totally qualified" to vote, just like every other warm body in the country, even if you can't even spell your own name. So let's, for the time being, forget about requiring "understanding," and simply focus on the requirement of "maturity."

When does a person become "mature"? Unless you are the aforementioned warm body, you are probably astute enough to see the similarity of *this* question to the question about the sky getting "dark." And, just as "day" does not mature into "night" at a point in time, so too does a "baby" not mature into an "adult" at any point in time. Instead, the question, "is (so-and-so) an adult yet?" will have an answer that is both "yes" to some degree, and "no" to some degree. (The *degree of maturity* for the person is merely that answer's degree of "yes.")

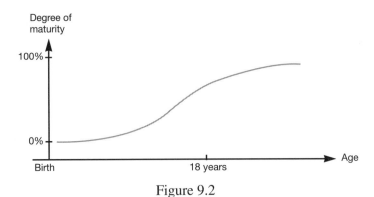

Figure 9.2

Of course we can "pretend" that maturity occurs at some point, such as 18, or 21, or some other fixed number of years. But rather than playing such games of "make-believe," let's instead look for a *realistic* solution to the voting issue. How can we

*Realistic Law* 149

use the *reality* of maturing (illustrated in Figure 9.2) to construct a Realistic law for voting?

The answer is obvious. In fact it utilizes the very same reasoning that we used in the park-trespassing example. (At any time, the *actual* fine for trespassing was some appropriate fraction of the *whole* fine.) Yet, almost everyone with whom I've ever discussed the matter of voting has had trouble seeing it at first. And the reason for the difficulty is that almost everyone mistakenly assumes that voting has to be an all-or-nothing process (i.e., either you *do* vote, or else you *don't* vote).

But just as we've acknowledged the concept of *partial guilt*, so too must we acknowledge the concept of *partial voting*. No, partial voting doesn't mean voting on only *some* of the items on the ballot. (Nor does it mean keeping at least some part of your body *outside* of the voting booth!) *Partial voting* means nothing more than assigning a *weight* to the vote. A weight of 100 percent would produce one whole vote, and a weight of 0 percent would be the equivalent of not voting at all. In fact this is exactly the way our voting laws *already* work! The only difference would be that partial voting would allow for additional possibilities besides just 0 percent and 100 percent.

Once the concept of a partial vote is acknowledged, we easily arrive at the:

### Realistic Voting Law:

**_Every_ citizen would have the right to vote. But each vote would be assigned a _weight_ equal to the degree of maturity of the voter.**

For example, a teenager with a 50 percent degree of maturity would have a vote that counts only half as much as an adult's vote. (So if the adult were to vote *for* an issue on the ballot, it would take two *half*-mature teenagers both voting *against* that issue to result in a wash.)

## 150    Shades of Reality

It's easy to see that the Realistic Voting Law fulfills the requirements of the Prime Directive of Equality. Any two voters of nearly identical age will always have nearly identical voting rights, regardless of their ages. There will be no point in time at which voting rights suddenly switch from "off" to "on."

You might be wondering, "So who's going to determine the *actual* 'degree of maturity' curve that is sketched in Figure 9.2"? Let me counter with a question of my own: "What 'degree of maturity' curve are we currently using right *now*"? The answer is shown in Figure 9.3. It's a step function with a discontinuity at 18 years of age. So who determined that *that* should be the curve for "maturity"?

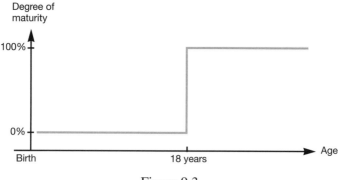

Figure 9.3

The "official" maturity curve might be determined by qualified psychologists or sociologists. Or we might establish the curve simply by *voting* for one. I don't so much care *how* the actual curve gets chosen, just as long as it's a "reasonable" curve. (The curve in Figure 9.3 is *not* "reasonable." It doesn't even *look* like reality.)

Even a quasi-realistic curve would be better than a step function. For example we might simply pick two different ages between which a person's voting rights "ramp up" from 0 percent to 100 percent, as suggested in Figure 9.4.

*Realistic Law* 151

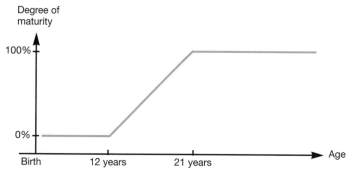

Figure 9.4

The Realistic Voting Law would be trivially easy to implement, even in our present society. When a person registers to vote, his/her birthday would be recorded by the registrar. On election day, all the ballots and the dates of birth of the corresponding voters would be put into the election computer. The computer would then simply multiply each vote by its corresponding degree of maturity before "counting" all the votes.

The notion of a weighted vote is not a new idea, nor is it even an "un-American" concept. In fact it's the very way publicly-held corporations hold elections at their stockholder meetings. Everybody who owns stock in the company does *not* get one vote identically equal to every other stockholder's vote. Instead, each vote is weighted in direct proportion to how much stock the voter owns. The more stock that a person has in the company, the more that person's vote counts. In a very similar sense, the Realistic Voting Law could then be interpreted as a reflection of how much "stock" each voter has in "maturity."

How mature should children have to be before we start teaching them the value of saving money? Should we require that a person be at least 18 years of age before we give them their first piggy bank? Of course not. We should encourage children to start appreciating the value of money long before that age, not

152    *Shades of Reality*

because their nickels and dimes are so intrinsically valuable, but because it helps to build responsible attitudes toward money. So too should it be with voting. What better way to start encouraging civic responsibility than to offer kids a voice (or more aptly, a "whisper") in our government, not because their tiny fractions of a vote would ever amount to anything significant, but because it would help build responsible attitudes toward government and society.

**Income Tax**

How might we incorporate the shades of gray concept to create a Realistic law for income tax? Paradoxically, our black and white, all-or-nothing legal system already *does* handle income tax Realistically! (At least it does so in *principle*.) For some unknown reason (perhaps in a rare moment of sanity), the lawmakers decided to implement a "sliding scale" tax law — the higher the income, the higher the tax. Had they decided to be consistent with the mentality they used in establishing the *voting* law, they might have come up with an all-or-nothing tax law like:

> Everyone whose annual income is *less* than 18 years of age (Oops!) I mean, less than 18,000 *dollars* pays absolutely *no* tax, and everyone whose annual income is *greater* than 18,000 dollars pays one fixed tax of $10,000.

**Parking in a "Red Zone"**

In California, if you park your car near a curb that is painted red, you are subject to receiving a parking ticket if any part of your car overlaps this "red zone." A friend of mine recently had this happen to her. "I was hardly even inside it," she said. "There couldn't have been more than ten inches of my car overlapping the red zone, and they *still* gave me a ticket."

There wasn't much I could do but agree with her. If she parked her car only *partially* inside the red zone, then she's only

*Realistic Law*     153

*partially guilty* of being in the red zone. It's not fair to "charge her" for the *entire* zone. If only ten inches of her car overlapped the red zone, then she was only about 5 percent guilty of illegally parking in it. Therefore, just like the person in Jackson Park who was only partially guilty of trespassing, she should have had to pay only 5 percent of the total fine. Of course the State of California (which doesn't acknowledge Realistic law) didn't see it that way. But then neither did my friend. According to her all-or-nothing reasoning, *most* of her car was *outside* of the red zone, so she felt that she shouldn't have to pay *anything*!

**Speeding**

The purpose of speed limits is to keep traffic moving at a safe rate of speed. But what is a "safe" speed? In general, the slower that all traffic moves, the safer everybody is. So the safest speed would be zero! (You can't very easily get into a traffic accident if nobody's moving.) Therefore, anybody driving at any non-zero speed is *already* unsafe to some degree. If one defines "speeding" as driving at an unsafe rate of speed, then *everyone* moving on the road is guilty of speeding to some *non*-zero degree! The question now becomes, how should all of these partial guilts be handled? It certainly wouldn't be practical (or socially acceptable) for police to stop absolutely everyone on the road and give them speeding tickets!

One interesting (even if somewhat impractical) idea might be to require all motor vehicles to carry the analog of an airline flight recorder in their trunks. Over the course of a year it would keep a constant record of each speed that the vehicle was driven. And since each road would have different location-dependent degrees of "safeness" for driving (for example, curves vs. straightaways), it would be necessary to record this location information as well. (This could be easily obtained from a Global Positioning Satellite navigation system.) Then, once a year, when it became time to renew the vehicle's registration, the recorder would be sent to the Department of Motor Vehicles and the owner would have to pay the accumulated total fines for the year.

A more practical (but less interesting) approach would be to adopt only a quasi-Realistic law — establish a maximum speed limit (similar to what we currently do). But then we would simply smooth out the fines so that they comply with the Prime Directive of Equality (see Figure 9.5).

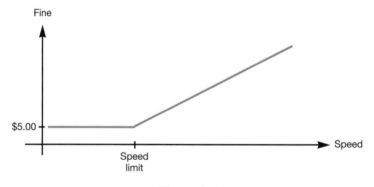

Figure 9.5

**Stop Signs**

While we're on the topic of safety and driving speed, do you *always* come to a full and complete stop whenever you reach an intersection controlled by a stop sign? Or do you sometimes slow down just enough to make sure that "the coast is clear" before continuing on? Conventional law says that you *must* come to a complete stop. But is such an extreme stop always really necessary? (Of course it's always *legally* necessary. But is it always *actually* necessary?)

A yield sign is similar to a stop sign, except that you are only required to slow down before proceeding. So there are at least *some* intersections where it is considered "safe" to merely

*Realistic Law* **155**

slow down before entering. In fact there are some "intersections" where it is actually safer not to even stop *at all*.

When California's Pasadena freeway (one of the first freeways in the United States) was built, its on-ramps were designed to have stop signs right at the point where the entering traffic was to merge with the rest of the freeway traffic! Today we know better than to require drivers to come to a complete stop before trying to merge into fast-moving traffic. It is actually safer to allow vehicles to *increase* their speed ("ramp-up") to match the flow of the main traffic before entering.

But this observation should apply not only to freeways, but to traffic in general. If you are driving on a road that is about to cross over a highway at an intersection that is controlled by a stop sign, you will spend more time in the intersection (and hence increase your risk of a collision) if you must first come to a dead stop, and *then* enter the intersection from a virtual standstill.

Whether or not you are required to stop at an intersection should be dictated by the traffic conditions that are present at the time, and not by a mindless sign sitting next to the road. You've got a brain. The sign *doesn't*. So use your common sense. If you are approaching an intersection that has a stop sign facing in your direction, and if traffic near (or already in) that intersection has the right-of-way, then you stop and wait your turn. But if you're approaching a stop sign at 3 o'clock in the morning, and if you've clearly determined that there isn't another vehicle or pedestrian in sight, then any law requiring you to continue slowing all the way down to a full and complete stop becomes nothing more than a stupid game and an insult to your intelligence.

In conclusion, we can state what should be the philosophy for all laws in general:

**Laws should present us with
guidelines, not boundary lines.**

156    *Shades of Reality*

### Consumption of Alcoholic Beverages

By going through a set of arguments virtually identical to those presented in the discussion of Realistic voting, we could develop what *appears* to be a Realistic law regarding the consumption of alcoholic beverages:

> *Everyone* should have the right to consume alcoholic beverages. But the amount that a person would be allowed to consume (over a given period of time) would be determined by his/her degree of maturity.

Such a law would have a slight problem, however. Perhaps you think that the problem might be how to *enforce* such a law. How would you prevent someone from simply visiting tavern after tavern and drinking his or her quota at each one?

There are many non-enforceable laws even in our present legal system. For example, murder is illegal — but how does the illegality of murder *prevent* murder? The answer is it doesn't. All it can do is make the wrongdoer suffer the consequences *after the fact*. So too with the above drinking law. So, non-enforceability is *not* the problem.

The trouble with the above law would be that it would once again present us with an Aristotelian boundary line between what would be "legal" and what would be "illegal." For any given age there would be a hard limit specifying how much alcohol is OK. It would require a person who drank slightly more than his/her legal limit to have to suffer the legal consequences, while another person who drank *almost* as much (but who stayed just *below* the legal limit) would be free of any legal consequences. This would violate the Prime Directive of Equality.

It's an easy mistake to make when using Aristotelian thinking to try and develop Realistic laws. Just remember one simple guideline when trying to develop a law governing a specific action: Always remember that the resulting law must be able to answer the question, "To what *degree* is the action legal"?

## Realistic Law 157

A Realistic drinking law is illustrated graphically in Figure 9.6. The degree of legality (vertical axis) of drinking a "fixed" amount of alcohol is presented as a function of age (horizontal axis). Different curves would exist for different "fixed" amounts of alcohol. Two such curves are shown in the figure.

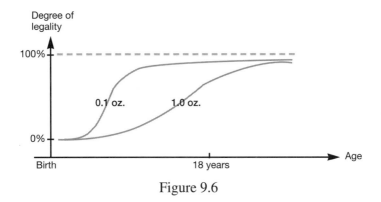

Figure 9.6

Notice, at any age, the more alcohol that a person consumes, the less legal that consumption becomes. However, there is no specific point at which they will have "reached their limit."

Also notice that, for any fixed amount of alcohol, the legality increases as the age increases. However, since alcohol is a drug, at no point does the legality ever reach 100 percent, except for the case of zero alcohol. (It's perfectly legal *not* to drink at *any* age!)

Similarly, we could construct "degree of legality" curves for other drugs such as marijuana, cocaine, etc. The legality curves for these drugs too would never reach the 100 percent mark. (Most of them wouldn't come close!) But just as with alcohol, there could be at least a *small* degree of legality to their use.

### Driving While Intoxicated

While we're on the subject of alcoholic consumption and the use of other such drugs, let's see how realism would affect

158    *Shades of Reality*

the law (in the previous chapter) that prohibits a person from driving a motor vehicle while intoxicated.

As was already pointed out, driving a vehicle at any non-zero speed (even when the driver is completely sober) is still dangerous to some degree. So driving while under the influence of alcohol is *really* inviting disaster. But if we still want to define "intoxicated" as having a blood alcohol content in excess of 0.08, then the degree of intoxication would define the degree of guilt. (For example, a blood alcohol level of 0.06 would imply a 75 percent degree of guilt, and a level of 0.08 or higher would imply 100 percent guilt.) Once again, any two similarly intoxicated drivers will have similar degrees of guilt (in accordance with the Prime Directive of Equality).

As the degree of intoxication continues to climb, the person might almost be regarded as being even "more than drunk." Certainly a person in such an extreme state of inebriation should not be allowed to enjoy the same privileges as someone who is merely "drunk" at the 0.08 level. We might therefore want to consider the possibility of extending the concept of degree of guilt to include values even *greater* than 100 percent.

I could continue going through all the laws, one by one, but that would be a boring exercise. Suffice it to say that virtually all of our present-day "black and white" laws could easily be modified into Realistic laws simply by remembering to specify degrees of legality, keeping in mind the Prime Directive of Equality, and applying common sense. The resulting laws, if properly derived, should then match the "spirits" of their corresponding Aristotelian counterparts, except that the sharp edges and corners would have been rounded off. Such laws would then conform to the Smoothness Principle of reality.

# Chapter Ten

# Legimetry

Because Realistic legal issues require more accurate specifications than simply "one" or "zero" (guilty or not guilty, legal or not legal, etc.), I have coined a new term, *Legimetry,* to define the field of study that deals with the *quantitative aspects of all legal issues.*

### Measuring vs. Counting

After a trial has ended you often hear reports like, "the defendant was found guilty of three counts of burglary." By the term "count," they mean the number of separate crimes for which the defendant was found guilty. But if all guilt is a matter of *degree*, then how does one "count" *fractions* of guilt?

The concepts of "counting" and "measuring" are very closely related. Both involve the determination of exactly "how much" of something exists. For example, if we have a bag full of identical marbles, and we want to know "how much" marbles we have, we simply count the number of *marbles*. But if we have a piece of string and we want to know "how much" string we have,

160    *Shades of Reality*

we can't simply count the number of *string*. (If we do, we'll always end up with *one*, regardless of the length of the string.) So instead, we mark off identical units of *length* (such as inches), and we then count *these* to determine "how much" string we have. Therefore, the concept of "measuring" is merely the concept of "counting" applied to *continua*. Measuring could be referred to as "fuzzy counting."

Let's say that you have been on a cross-country driving trip and you want to know what kind of gas mileage you got with your car. Would you simply *count* the total number of times that you stopped to buy gas? While this might give you a crude estimate of your gas mileage, it would have been more meaningful to have kept track of the total number of *gallons* that you purchased on the trip. And this total amount of gasoline is independent of how many times you choose to stop and buy it. You could just as easily have stopped for gas *twice* as often. But then you would have bought only *half* as much at each stop.

Perhaps you've heard the joke about the fellow who went into an Italian restaurant and ordered a pizza. "How would you like your pizza sliced?" asked the cook, "into eight pieces, or twelve pieces"? After thinking for a moment the customer replied, "You'd better slice it into *eight* pieces. I don't think I'm hungry enough to eat *twelve* pieces."

Obviously, the net amount of an entity is independent of how you choose to divide it. I recently saw a TV commercial by a loan company that *did* try to give the impression that it *wasn't*. According to the commercial, a person could easily solve all her financial problems by simply applying for one of their loans and using the money to pay off all her bills. Then, instead of having to make *many* payments each month, the person would only have to make *one* monthly payment!

### "Three Strikes" Laws

If you had a pile of gold nuggets (each of a different size) and you wanted to determine the total amount of gold in the pile,

*Legimetry*     161

you wouldn't simply *count the number* of nuggets. Instead you would more realistically *measure the weights* of all the nuggets, since "amount of gold" is a concept that forms a continuum.

Since guilt and levels of crime also exist on continua, we cannot simply "count" them *either* (not if we expect to arrive at any kind of meaningful interpretation). For example if we try to implement a "three-strikes-and-you're-out" type of law, we immediately get bogged down in the question of deciding which crimes *should* be "counted" as strikes and which ones *shouldn't*. (If you have "three coins," do you have sufficient funds to purchase a fifty-cent candy bar? The answer depends on what three coins you have!) Time after time, judges are finding criminals guilty of a third strike. But then appeals are filed attempting to discard one of the previous crimes as not being "bad enough" to warrant the full Three Strikes penalty. They claim that the "strike" was merely a "foul ball." (It is somewhat revealing that such baseball-type terminology should be used in these matters, because it helps to underscore the realization that our contemporary legal system *is* nothing more than a foolish *game*!)

The problem with Three Strikes laws is that they quantify crimes incorrectly. Crimes need to be *measured*, not simply *counted*. All crimes are not equally bad. While there is probably no such thing as a "good crime," some are certainly better than others. For example, murder is worse than robbery, and robbery is worse than jaywalking. Each one represents a different *level* of crime, and that amount needs to be quantified.

### Crimes of Theft

Let's begin with a very simple example. Suppose a man steals $100 from a bank. The *crime* is therefore "the theft of $100." It doesn't matter whether the theft occurred as a single theft of $100, or as two separate thefts of $50 each, or even as 100 separate thefts of $1 each. The crime remains "the theft of $100" regardless of how that total amount was reached.

162    *Shades of Reality*

Notice that I used the singular form of the word, "crime" (not crimes), even if multiple thefts are involved. Traditional all-or-nothing law declares that each separate theft is a totally new separate crime. But if you adopt such a traditional viewpoint, then where do you "draw the line" between one theft and another *separate* theft? Suppose the man picked up the $100, one $1 bill at a time. Should this be considered to be 100 individual thefts? Suppose he even separately carried each $1 bill out to his car parked in front of the bank. *Now* should it be considered to be 100 separate thefts? How long must the man wait before going back inside the bank to get the next dollar bill in order for its theft to be considered a completely *new* theft? Legimetry doesn't have to deal with these kinds of questions because it *measures* crime instead of *counting* it.

### Level of Crime for Theft

In order to quantify crimes, we need to define a way of numerically specifying their amounts of "badness." This numerical value would then define the *Level of Crime* (in terms of *crime units*) for that particular crime.

> **For thefts, the level of crime is simply defined to be the total dollar amount (of money or merchandise) that was stolen.**

Therefore, in our above example, the level of crime for the bank theft(s) would be *100 crime units*.

As we have already discussed, we cannot (in general) "count" the number of individual thefts that were committed. And so the penalty imposed on a criminal for the commission of a theft(s) should be simply proportional to the level of crime corresponding to the theft(s). (I'm aware that this *isn't* the way it's currently done.)

*Legimetry*     163

For example if the above bank robber gets caught, his prison sentence should be only half as long as another "identical" robber who commits 200 crime units by stealing $200. However, since all robbers are *not* "identical," all thefts of a given dollar amount need *not* necessarily have identical penalties. In other words, if two different robbers each steal $100, they might *not* both receive identical prison sentences. I will discuss this further later in this chapter.

Perhaps you feel that the actual dollar amount of a theft is not what's important. Instead, maybe you feel that the mere fact that *any* amount was stolen is sufficient to call it "a crime," regardless of how much money is actually involved. In other words, the fact that a person has *"committed"* (i.e., made a *commitment* to) a theft is all that matters. (It's kind of a *mind* thing.)

Then consider a person who enters a bank with every intention of stealing as much money as he can. (In his mind there is absolutely *no doubt* about what he intends to do — he has made the commitment to rob the bank when nobody's looking.) But try as he may, he just can't seem to find a way to get into the vault without being seen. So he eventually leaves the bank after having stolen a total of zero dollars. Would you say that he was "guilty" of committing a theft crime? (As the old saying goes, you can't go to jail for what you're thinking.) But if the dollar amount of a theft crime is unimportant, then, according to you, a person is "guilty" of theft regardless of whether he steals one hundred dollars, one dollar, or *zero* dollars!

Failure to acknowledge the concept of *level* of crime forces you into the awkward Aristotelian position of having to "draw the line at zero" by unrealistically declaring that the only distinction between the "category" called *non-crime* and the "category" called *crime* is whether the amount stolen is either *zero* dollars or *more than* zero dollars.

164     *Shades of Reality*

## Conservation of Crime and Guilt

When a law is broken, a crime is established that must be accounted for. When the person (or persons) responsible for the crime is finally convicted, their guilts must exactly balance the crime that was committed. There cannot have been more crime committed than there are guilts (unless some of the criminals have still not yet been apprehended). Nor can there be more guilts than there was crime (unless some of the criminals are guilty of "nothing").

To illustrate, let's look at three slightly different burglary cases, all involving the theft of television sets:

### Case 1:

A burglar breaks into somebody's home and steals a television set. The crime is therefore "the theft of one television set." Soon after the theft, the burglar is apprehended, brought to trial, and convicted. He is found guilty of stealing one television set. *One* theft of a TV is exactly balanced by *one* guilt. Case closed.

### Case 2:

A burglar breaks into someone's house and steals a TV set, and another burglar down the street breaks into somebody else's home and also steals a television set. The crime is therefore "the theft of two television sets." Both burglars are caught and convicted. Each burglar is found guilty of stealing one television set. *Two* thefts of TVs are exactly balanced by *two* guilts. Case closed.

### Case 3:

Two burglars *working together* break into a home and jointly steal one television set. The crime is therefore "the theft

*Legimetry*     165

of one television set." Both burglars are caught and convicted. Is each burglar guilty of stealing the TV set?

The total guilts must match the total crime that was committed. In Case 2, the *two* guilts (each of stealing *one* TV) exactly match the crime (the theft of *two* television sets). But in Case 3, if *both* burglars were to be found guilty of stealing the *one* TV, then this verdict would represent exactly the same verdict as in Case 2 where the crime was *different* (the theft of *two* television sets). There would be a mismatch.

A court of law cannot create crime and guilt "out of thin air." (Only a criminal can do that!) A court of law cannot just "pretend" that the crime was "the theft of *two* television sets" when in actuality only *one* was stolen. Therefore, *both* burglars cannot each be 100 percent guilty of stealing the *one* TV.

One realistic verdict for Case 3 would be that the two burglars were each *50 percent* guilty of stealing the television set (assuming that they were both equally involved in the planning and commission of the crime). Another equally valid verdict would be that each burglar was 100 percent guilty of stealing only *half* of the TV. Either way,

*the sum of the products of the individual guilts* ($g_i$) *times the individual crimes* ($c_i$) *must exactly equal the total crime that was actually committed:*

$$\text{Total Crime} = g_1 c_1 + g_2 c_2 + \cdots + g_n c_n \, ,$$

where:

$$n = \text{the number of criminals.}$$

I refer to the above principle as the **Conservation of Crime and Guilt.** In essence it simply says that the level of crime (for any specific crime) is a fixed amount. And the person(s) who commits that crime cannot be "guiltier" than the total level of

166    *Shades of Reality*

guilt that must be accounted for.

I realize that these concepts are completely foreign to the American legal system's all-or-nothing approach to law. So perhaps another example or two will help to clarify the concepts.

### Example 1 — Three Equal Robbers

Suppose three men equally participate in a bank robbery. They steal a total of $750,000 in cash from the bank. If caught, what charges should be brought against each man?

> Answer 1: Each man could be charged with 33⅓ percent of the entire crime of stealing $750,000. If convicted, each would then be 33⅓ percent guilty of stealing the entire $750,000.

> Answer 2: Each man could be charged with separately stealing $250,000. If convicted, each would then be 100 percent guilty of stealing his separate $250,000.

Answers 1 and 2 are legimetrically equivalent, and so the prison sentences associated with either answer would be identical, assuming that prison sentences are allocated in direct proportion to crime level (which they *should* be). So, if a person is only ⅓ guilty of a crime, then that person's penalty should be only ⅓ of the *total* penalty for the crime.

### Example 2 — Two Unequal Robbers

It is not a requirement that each participant in the crime must have equal involvement in the crime. For example, consider the following scenario:

Two burglars break into a house together. One burglar goes upstairs to see what he can find while his partner remains down-

*Legimetry* 167

stairs. The upstairs burglar finds a $20 bill on a small table in the bedroom. Seeing that his partner isn't around, the burglar secretly hides the money in his pocket to keep for himself.

Meanwhile, the downstairs burglar has just found a $50 bill hidden away in a drawer in the downstairs den. Being just as honorable as his partner, he too slips the cash away in a secret pocket in his coat.

Not being able to find anything else of value, the two men finally decide to leave the house. But just to keep their night's escapade from being a total failure, they decide to steal the living room sofa. However, before they can make a clean getaway, they are caught. What charges should be brought against each man?

> Answer 1: The upstairs burglar should be charged with stealing $20. The downstairs burglar should be charged with stealing $50. Each burglar could be charged with 1/2 of the entire crime of stealing the sofa. If convicted, the upstairs burglar would be 100 percent guilty of stealing $20, and 50 percent guilty of stealing the entire sofa. The downstairs burglar would be 100 percent guilty of stealing $50, and 50 percent guilty of stealing the entire sofa.

> Answer 2: Just as in Answer 1, each burglar would be 100 percent guilty of his own private monetary theft. In addition, each burglar would be 100 percent guilty of stealing *half* of the sofa.

Actually there could be an infinite number of answers to these kinds of questions. For example, the upstairs burglar in the last scenario could be charged with stealing $100, but he would only be 20 percent guilty of that accusation. Or he might even be considered 200 percent guilty of stealing $10, or 400 percent guilty of stealing $5, etc. Legimetrically, it makes no difference

168     *Shades of Reality*

how you choose to slice the pie, just as long as you remember to adhere to the Conservation of Crime and Guilt.

## Non-theft Crimes

Up until now we have considered only crimes that have involved thefts of money or merchandise. In these cases it is fairly trivial to establish numerical values for the levels of crime. (They are simply equal to the dollar amounts that were stolen, or the fair market values of the merchandise that was taken.) But what about crimes like murder, rape, or kidnapping? How can we assign numerical values to the levels of crime for these types of *non*-theft crimes?

At first thought it might seem like attempting to compare a crime like theft to a crime like rape (or murder, kidnapping, etc.) might be like trying to compare apples with oranges. But apples and oranges *can* be compared, at least in terms of their costs. For example, if apples sell for 39 cents apiece and oranges sell for 59 cents apiece, then three apples are approximately equal to two oranges, at least in terms of their consequences to your pocketbook.

Similarly, we can quantify crimes in terms of how much it "costs" to commit them. Since (in an ideal system) the penalty for committing any crime should be directly proportional to the level of crime, we can work backwards and use this penalty information to deduce the level of crime that would have warranted the given penalty.

The following table (compiled from the 1996 edition of the California Penal Codes) lists some representative crimes and their corresponding penalties as defined by our present legal system:

| Crime | Penalty |
| --- | --- |
| Murder (1st degree) | 25 years – life |
| Murder (2nd degree) | 15 years – life |
| Manslaughter | 3 – 11 years |
| Robbery (1st degree) | 3 – 9 years |
| Kidnapping | 3 – 8 years |
| Rape | 3 – 8 years |
| Burglary | 2 – 6 years |
| Arson | 2 – 6 years |
| Robbery (2nd degree) | 2 – 5 years |
| Assault (with a deadly weapon) | 2 – 4 years |
| Grand theft (and automobile theft) | 16 months – 3 years |
| Vandalism | 1/2 – 1 year |
| Forgery | less than 1 year |
| Possession of marijuana | less than 1 year |
| Trespassing | less than 1/2 year |
| Petty theft* ( less than $400 ) | less than 1/2 year |

The *precise* specifications of levels of crime for the items in the above table will be one of the tasks for future legimetricians. But we can make at least a *crude* attempt at trying to determine the values, based on how our legal system currently assesses the consequences of committing those crimes (as shown in column two of the above table).

First we will need to determine an approximate value for the ratio: number of stolen dollars per month of prison term. We will use the items, "Grand theft" and "Petty theft" to estimate this ratio. (Of course the Penal Code does not spell out specific

---

*("Petty theft" is Aristotelianly defined as a theft of less than $400. So if you ever plan to steal $400 and you want to avoid the complications associated with having committed a "major" crime, you'd better be sure to leave a penny behind so that the total theft becomes only $399.99!)

170 *Shades of Reality*

dollar amounts for thefts. It merely lumps all thefts into pseudo-categories of "less than $400" vs. "greater than $400." So our analysis will only yield a "ballpark" estimate.)

An "average" automobile on the street today is probably worth about a few thousand dollars (give or take). And the penalty for stealing an automobile (Grand theft) is a few years in prison (16 months to 3 years). So, to a first approximation, the penalty for stealing each $1,000 is the equivalent of about one year in prison (or about one month for every $100), based on the penalty for Grand theft.

Similarly, if someone steals only a few hundred dollars (less than $400) he will be guilty of Petty theft, and he will be incarcerated for a few months (less than half a year). Once again, the result comes out to about one month for every $100 that was stolen.

Therefore, we have now determined (to a crude approximation) that the ratio of stolen dollars to months in prison is roughly 100 to 1. We might use this ratio to specify the legimetric *guideline* that:

> *The penalty for theft should be about one year in prison for every $1,000 that is stolen (or equivalently, about one day for every $3).*

### Level of Crime (for Non-Theft)

We are now in a position to determine, for *any* specified crime, the numerical value of its level of crime. Simply:

> **Calculate how many dollars you would need to steal in order to be assigned the same penalty as committing the specified crime.**

The resulting dollar amount will be numerically equal to the number of crime units constituting the level of crime.

*Legimetry*     171

For example how much money would a person have to steal in order to commit a crime that was "just as bad" as rape? The answer: $3,000–$8,000. (Because the penalty for rape is 3–8 years in prison, and each year in prison is equivalent to the penalty of stealing about $1,000.) Therefore, the level of crime for a rape would be somewhere between 3,000 and 8,000 crime units.

A quick rule of thumb for our previous table of crimes would be to simply interpret the right-hand column as indicating "thousands of crime units" instead of "years." (But just remember — the ratio of 1000 to 1 is only a crude approximation.)

### A Better Way To "Strike Out"

As was pointed out at the beginning of this chapter, crimes need to be *measured*, not simply *counted*. So one simple improvement in a "Three Strikes" law might be to merely keep a running *sum* of the *total crime units* that a criminal has accumulated on his record. When this amount exceeds some specified maximum, the criminal will have "struck out."

For example legimetricians might set a value like 5,000 as the maximum allowable crime units that any criminal is allowed to accumulate. If the criminal has previously been convicted of Arson (2,000 crime units), a $700 theft (700 crime units), and Assault (2,000 crime units), he would still have 300 crime units to go before he "strikes out."

Even doing no more than this would be a substantial improvement over our current "Three Strikes" laws. There would no longer be any debate about which crimes should or shouldn't "count" as a strike. They would *all* "count," but to different degrees, depending on the level of each crime.

But this new way of "striking out" (just like the present way) would still violate the Prime Directive of Equality. Criminals would still be presented with a hard Aristotelian boundary

172 *Shades of Reality*

line separating "striking out" from "not striking out." A criminal with 5,001 crime units on his record would be put away, while one with 4,999 would still be free.

### "Fading Out"

The best solution to the problem is not to let criminals "*strike* out," but to let them "*fade* out." Instead of striking out all-or-nothing, they could strike out "a little bit at a time." All this would mean is that, instead of assigning *fixed* penalties for crimes (such as our guideline of one day in prison for every 3 crime units committed), we let the penalty (per crime unit) be determined by the criminal's *past record*. So a first offender might receive the standard penalty (one prison day per 3 crime units). But as he continues to accumulate crime units in the future, the penalty per crime unit would gradually increase and increase, until he finally ends up finding himself in prison all the time. And there would have been no single crime unit which put him "over the line." He would have just "faded out of society," and "faded into prison," for life.

"Fading out" would have the advantage that the more hardened criminals would be treated more severely than first-time offenders. Proven lawbreakers would therefore not be getting off so lightly. But fading out would also have the additional benefit in that it would adhere to the Prime Directive of Equality. Any two criminals with nearly identical criminal records would always receive nearly equal prison terms for committing nearly equal crimes.

### The Specification of Realistic Laws

As we have seen, Realistic laws are often expressed as curves (or tables of numbers) indicating the degrees of legality of specific issues. For example, the law governing the consumption

*Legimetry*      173

of alcoholic beverages was a set of curves (see Figure 9.6) expressing the legality of consuming a specified amount of alcohol by a person of any given age. (These curves would therefore define the "level of crime" that would be committed whenever a person of any particular age were to consume the specified amount of alcohol.) The precise specification of these kinds of curves (or tables) would be the task of legimetricians.

However, legimetry is not limited to merely the measurement of crime. Legimetry deals with the quantitative aspects of *all* legal issues. Therefore, the specification of curves, such as the "degree of maturity" curve (which we saw in Figure 9.2 in conjunction with our discussion about voting rights), would also fall under the domain of Legimetry.

To be sure, Realistic laws and Legimetry are a little more complicated than the simpleminded "yes or no" laws that we currently use. (By the same token, mathematics would have been easier if the value of *pi* could have been simply *3* instead of an irrational number!) But then reality has to be whatever it *is*, even if that reality "sucks" (to quote from a poster that I once saw).

Of course we can always just go on *pretending* anything we want and hope that reality doesn't get in the way. But that approach doesn't always work, as we will see in the next chapter.

# Chapter Eleven

# Abortion

Even having read through this much of the book, a dyed-in-the-wool pragmatic Aristotelian might still say, "So what! All of this business about smoothing out step functions and creating Realistic laws is all just a lot of humbug! So what, if we draw the line at 18 as the minimum voting age? So what, if our laws violate your silly Prime Directive of Equality? Who cares? The way we currently do things in this country is just fine, because it all works. And if something works, don't fix it!"

Well, we are now going to discuss a topic for which the current Aristotelian way of thinking does *not* "work just fine." It's an issue that the "draw-the-line" mentality does *not* resolve *at all*. I am referring to the subject of abortion.

It may be easy to dismiss questions about what time the sky gets dark as being frivolous and unimportant. And it may be only of academic interest that a lightbulb requires a small but finite amount of time to turn on. In these instances, we can just ignore the truth and, for all practical purposes, simply pretend that they happen instantaneously. We can pretend because such simplifications do not have any profound life-or-death consequences.

174

*Abortion*    175

But when it comes to pregnancy, we can no longer ignore reality. We *cannot* make reality "easier" by simply "pretending" that a fully-grown person suddenly "pops out" of a woman's body at the instant of conception. There is no denying that pregnancy is a *prolonged* period of time lasting many months. And there just isn't any way that we can make this fact conveniently "go away."

The abortion issue, therefore, stands full square in the face of the bivalent mentality and challenges it for a solution. And none is forthcoming — because *the Aristotelian framework is the wrong paradigm in which to look for a solution.* One cannot be expected to decide which of two possible answers to a question is the correct answer when both of those answers are wrong! One of the crowning achievements of fuzzy logic, therefore, may be that it finally presents the tools for resolving the abortion issue once and for all.

Before we begin applying fuzzy logic to the abortion issue, let me first preface my discussion with an important statement: *I am completely neutral on the matter of abortion.* I view the entire abortion issue as being merely an interesting intellectual exercise. And so I am able to approach the subject without any personal biases or hidden "agenda" as to what I would *like* the final outcome on the abortion matter to be.

Let's begin by looking at the main ideas currently expressed by the two existing dominant camps, the so-called "pro-lifers" and the so-called "pro-choicers."

### The Anti-abortion (or "Pro-life") View

The anti-abortion group likes to refer to itself as being "pro-life," which presumably means "pro-*all*life." (If they had meant only *human* life, then they would have explicitly said "pro-*human*life." But they didn't. Therefore, *all* life, both plant and animal, must be sacred to them.) This must leave them with quite

176     *Shades of Reality*

an interesting dilemma of trying to decide what to eat! I therefore prefer to refer to this group more properly as the "anti-abortion" group.

The anti-abortionists are of the frame of mind that a human being comes into existence at the "moment of conception." The reason for this belief stems from a sorites-type of argument. They reason: if a baby is a human being when it is born, then it must have also been a human being one minute before it was born, and then one minute before that, etc. Continuing this reasoning process backwards in time to the "point of conception," they can find no magical point in time at which anything of significance occurs to mark the start of being human. Since conception itself appears to be the only clear-cut "discontinuity" that they can identify, it must be (in the anti-abortionist opinion) at *that* time that the transition from *non*-human being to 100 percent human being is made, and at that time the "soul" enters the "person." (We will discuss the concept of souls further when we get to Chapter Thirteen.)

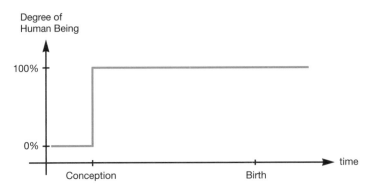

Figure 11.1 — The Anti-Abortionist's Paradigm

However, as we know from the Smoothness Principle (see Chapter One), conception does not occur at a precise "point in time." How should one define the exact "moment" of concep-

*Abortion*    177

tion? When the sperm first "touches" the egg? When it's halfway inside? What defines the last split second of time at which the egg could (in principle) be destroyed without it being called the killing of a baby? Anti-abortionists have a tough time dealing with these kinds of questions, and so they usually just brush them aside as being irrelevant. (A few years ago I hosted a debate at KSCO radio on the abortion issue, and when I pressed the "prolifer" to discuss these issues, he threatened to walk out of the studio unless I changed the subject!)

Another argument advanced by anti-abortionists is that a fetus is to be considered as being a human being because if it is allowed to continue growing, it will eventually *become* one. The problem with this kind of argument is that it avoids focusing on the *current* reality. Someday the fetus might even grow up to adulthood and eventually die of old age. It should therefore be just as valid to argue that a fetus is *presently a cadaver* since, if it is allowed to continue growing, it would eventually become one!

### The Pro-Abortion (or "Pro-Choice") View

The Pro-abortion group likes to refer to itself as being "prochoice." I too like to make choices — I choose which clothes I will wear, at which restaurant I will eat lunch, etc. In fact, I would suspect that most anti-abortionists like to make these very same kinds of choices *too*! Therefore, even anti-abortionists are pro-"choice." Furthermore, everyone has the "choice" of whether or not they should become a shoplifter, for example. (They have the *choice*, providing they are also willing to accept the *consequences*!) But the issue at hand is not one of making *choices*. The issue at hand is *abortion*. Therefore, I prefer to refer to this group more properly as the "pro-abortion" group.

The pro-abortionists are of the frame of mind that a fetus doesn't become a human being until some *future* time (usually measured in terms of something called "trimesters"). At that

## 178    Shades of Reality

point in time, some supposedly invisible and magical process instantly turns the fetus into a 100 percent human being. After that magical instant, it is no longer OK to have an abortion performed. (But one hour *prior* to the that moment, it apparently *is* OK!) The trouble is, none of the pro-abortionists can seem to agree on just *what* or *when* this magical event is. So they all just make up their *own* rules depending on what turns out to be convenient for themselves.

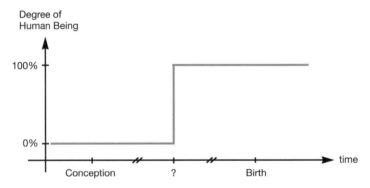

Figure 11.2 — The Pro-Abortionist's Paradigm

    A common pro-abortionist defense of their position (especially when discussing their views with a male) is: "You're not the one who's pregnant, and so you're not qualified to comment on the subject!" Of course that kind of reasoning would imply that a botanist is not qualified to discuss the subject of *plants*, simply because she *herself* is not a *plant*!
    And finally, pro-abortionists argue that "nobody has the right to tell a woman what she can and cannot do with her *own body*." But if an object inside of a woman's body is to be regarded as being a *part* of her own body, then if a woman were to walk into a jewelry store and swallow a diamond ring, who would be the legal owner of that ring!?
    (Actually, the claim that a fetus is a part of the woman's

*Abortion*     179

body *may* in reality be partially *valid*. I will return to this point shortly.)

### What is a "Human Being"?

Gray" represents a color in which both "black" and "white" are each present to some degree. The less black in the mixture, the lighter the shade of gray. If no black whatsoever is present, then the shade of gray is called "100 percent white," (or just plain "white"). Since there is no more black that can be removed, this level of whiteness is as white as anything can get. (And there actually are substances, such as magnesium oxide, which come very close to being 100 percent white.) Therefore, "whiteness" is a concept which, in addition to being *bounded,* is nearly absolutely attainable in the real world.

But even though they rhyme and have functional similarities, it's important not to confuse "whiteness" with "brightness." Brightness is *not* something which is ever achievable or attainable in an absolute sense. Even the sun is not as bright as something can possibly be. In fact there is *no* object that you can point to and say, "This object is 100 percent bright." The term "brightness" (unlike "whiteness") is an *unbounded* concept. Any light can (at least in principle) become just a little bit brighter than it currently is.

The term, "human being" is very much like "brightness." Both represent unbounded concepts whose levels of existence can only be specified in terms of degrees. You cannot point to any living entity on this planet and say, "That is a 100 percent human being," any more than you can point to a light that is 100 percent bright. There is always room for "improvement" in both cases. And if mankind should continue to exist and develop for another million years, will it become *more* than human? Or might it turn out in retrospect that we, of today, will have been merely *less* than human?

180     *Shades of Reality*

We might be tempted to view present-day "human-ness" in *comparative* terms relative to some *physical* criterion. For example, we *can* specify to what degree an entity's DNA conforms to that of the species, Homo sapiens. But if we try to use *that* as measure of "human-ness" then even a woman's *unfertilized* egg (or even a strand of her *hair*, or a drop of her blood) would qualify as being a "human being."

One of the problems with trying to perceive "human-ness" in terms of shades of gray is that, apart from relatively rare exceptions, most of us are fairly "normal," and therefore we have a kind of sameness to us. Except for petty individual differences, we all pretty much look and act and think like every other member of our species. We all have hopes, fears, joys, and sorrows. We all experience these kinds of emotions, which we feel make us "human." And so most of us probably cluster around a "human-ness level" near the 100 percent mark. (At least it would appear that way to *us*, not currently having any higher life forms to compare ourselves to.) And so there is the Aristotelian inclination to "round off" everybody and pretend that the slight differences in levels of "human-ness" from one person to another simply don't exist. In short, we *equify* ourselves.

Another problem with trying to understand the shades of gray of "human-ness" stems from our religious upbringings. Most religions are inherently Aristotelian in their dogmas. (God must have not known about fuzzy logic back then!) Consequently, we are led to believe that whenever you do something, either you have committed a sin or else you haven't sinned at all. Either you are a good person or else you are a bad person. Either you'll go to heaven when you die, or else you'll go to hell. And if you're a human being, then you are created in God's image. And if you *are* created in His image, then you are created in that image all-or-nothing.

But if something is only *almost* a human being, then in whose image is it created? Religion can't answer these kinds of questions about degrees of human-ness because religion never thought about them. To the bivalent religious mind, every person is simply a "human being," and everything else is *not*. Period. Case closed. (And *mind* closed, as well!)

We will return to the discussion of religion's perceptions of reality in Chapter Thirteen when we discuss the concepts of death, heaven, hell, and souls.

### The "Pro-Reality" View

I will now define a *third* point of view for the abortion issue. The pro-*reality* view bases its analysis on the reality that an embryo *gradually* makes the transition from *non*-human to more *nearly* human over an extended period of time (many months). Therefore at any point in time it can be regarded as being both a human being (to some degree) and not a human being (to some degree), as shown in Figure 11.3.

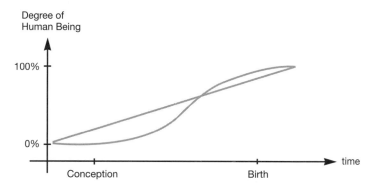

Figure 11.3 — The Pro-Reality Paradigm

Using this "degree of human being" curve, we can now answer the question, "to what degree does an abortion constitute killing a human being"? The exact answer, of course, depends on how long after conception the abortion is performed. The later

182     *Shades of Reality*

the abortion, the greater the degree of guilt of killing a human being. (The arguments are exactly the same as those that we developed in Chapter Nine when we discussed the example of the park trespasser.)

## The Kingdom of Fairenjust

Once upon a time there was a kingdom named Fairenjust, in which all of the citizens were ruled with a policy of fairness and equality for everyone. The underlying philosophy governing the Fairenjustian judicial system was a simple Prime Directive of Equality:

> In a court of law, any two virtually identical crimes *must* result in virtually equal judgments by the court.

Any judge who failed to comply with this Prime Directive would be immediately banished from the kingdom forever.

Many years ago when the king was just a little boy, he became lost in the woods and couldn't find his way out. Just when everything seemed hopeless, a beautiful orange and black butterfly suddenly appeared and led the boy safely back to his home. In gratitude, his father issued a royal decree that, henceforth, all such butterflies would forever be under the protection of the Royal Court. Anyone found guilty of killing such a "Monarch" butterfly would be automatically sentenced to one year imprisonment in the Royal dungeon.

However, caterpillars were an entirely different matter. Since they infested the flowers and the gardens of the kingdom, they were regarded as nothing more than common ordinary pests. And so it was *not* considered a crime to kill a caterpillar.

One day Mr. Chang Wo, a citizen of oriental descent, was out working in his garden. Now Mr. Wo was not *at all* a clumsy man, someone with "two left feet." (In fact, Mr. Wo was so much *not* clumsy that he actually had two *right* feet!) However, on this

*Abortion*     183

particular day, Mr. Chang Wo had forgotten to wear his glasses, and he accidentally stepped on a butterfly cocoon, squishing it to death with his two right feet. A member of the Royal Academy's Department of Entomology (RADE) witnessed the event and immediately arrested Mr. Chang Wo and charged him with the crime of killing a Royal Butterfly. Mr. Wo, however, claimed it was not a butterfly *at all*. He claimed that it was only a caterpillar in a cocoon.

The trial dragged on for many months. But in the end, the Fairenjustian Supreme Court issued its famous "Wo vs. RADE" landmark decision, which ruled in favor of "The Wo man's right two shoes."

Because of the Prime Directive of Equality, the Supreme Court ruling therefore applied to all of the *other* citizens in the kingdom as well. Anyone could destroy a *cocoon* if they so chose.

But many of the citizens were squeamish and abhorred the messy idea of having to *squish* their own cocoons out of existence. So a more humane way was devised in which a technician would first "bore" a tiny hole in the cocoon with a small drill. He would then "shine" a laser beam through the hole to kill the cocoon's contents. This "bore-shine" method was clean and effective and, before long, bore-shine clinics started springing up everywhere in the kingdom.

One day a woman brought two virtually identical cocoons into a bore-shine clinic. The technician performed a bore-shine procedure on the first cocoon without any difficulty. But before he could finish the bore-shine procedure on the second cocoon, the butterfly had already started emerging before being killed by the laser beam. Both the woman and the technician were immediately arrested, charged with the crime of killing a butterfly, and sentenced to one year in the Royal Dungeon.

When the king heard about the convictions, he was outraged. Two virtually identical cocoons had been destroyed, but

184    *Shades of Reality*

the destruction of one of the cocoons was ruled to be *legal*, while the destruction of the other virtually identical cocoon was condemned as a *crime*. This was a clear and flagrant violation of the kingdom's Prime Directive. The presiding judge was immediately banished from the kingdom, and he took refuge in a legislatively backward little country known as the United States, where his primitive bivalent mentality was not only *tolerated* but was actually accepted without question.

Meanwhile, back in the kingdom of Fairenjust, the king had assembled a *new* Royal Court and once again warned them against violating the Prime Directive — virtually identical crimes *must* result in virtually equal court judgments.

The new court was quick to reverse the Wo vs. RADE decision, and thereby declared that all cocoons now contain *butterflies* and *not* caterpillars. However, this decision also ended up violating the Prime Directive one day when a woman killed two virtually identical caterpillars, one of which had just *entered* its cocoon and the other of which was just *about* to enter its cocoon.

The Royal Court was now in a real quandary. If they assumed the cocoon contained a *caterpillar*, it led to a violation of the Prime Directive. But if they assumed that the cocoon contained a *butterfly*, that *too* led to a violation of the Prime Directive. They were becoming desperate for a solution.

One day a wise and noble scholar, Mr. Cigol, rode into the kingdom. Mr. Cigol visited the Royal Court and proclaimed that he had a solution to their problem. "Since you have a kind of *'fuzzy'* caterpillar dilemma, why don't you just apply *'fuzzy'* logic to the problem"?

The members of the Royal Court laughed and laughed. *"Fuzzy"* logic indeed!

But Mr. Cigol was a patient man and continued explaining. "Instead of pretending that a cocoon always contains a caterpillar or pretending that a cocoon always contains a butterfly, why not stop *pretending* and just view the matter *realistically*."

## Abortion 185

"A cocoon starts out containing a caterpillar," he continued, "and ends up containing a butterfly. The change from caterpillar to butterfly does not occur at any particular point in time. Instead, the transition occurs *gradually* through a process called *metamorphosis* in which the contents of the cocoon at any instant can be regarded as being *both* a caterpillar (to some degree), *and* a butterfly (also to some degree)."

"When a fetus . . ." (Oops, I mean *cocoon*.) "When a cocoon is killed, only a part-butterfly entity is killed. The killer therefore is only partly (but not completely) guilty of killing a butterfly. So, in the absence of any extenuating circumstances, the killer should therefore be required to suffer part (but not all) of the penalty for killing a complete butterfly. The closer the contents of the cocoon resemble a complete butterfly, the more severe the penalty should be."

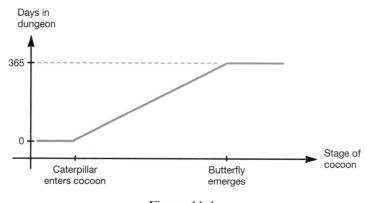

Figure 11.4

"In this way the entire matter is treated fairly and realistically, and the Prime Directive of Equality need never be violated. It's as simple as that."

The members of the Fairenjustian Royal Court stared at Mr. Cigol in astonishment and wonder. "Fuzzy logic"! they thought.

## 186    *Shades of Reality*

"Hmmm. . . *Fuzzy* logic?" they wondered. *"Fuzzy logic? Fuzzy* (Smr-r-f-f-t, Heh-heh) **logic**?! Ha-ha! HE-HEE-HO!"

They never heard of anything so silly!

Of course, a human fetus is not *exactly* analogous to a butterfly cocoon. There are definite dissimilarities between the two. For example, one of the obvious major differences is that a fetus lives inside a woman's body, whereas a cocoon does not. Therefore the pro-abortionists may have a somewhat legitimate argument when they claim that a fetus is actually a part of a woman's body, and as such, the woman has the right to deal with the matter privately.

However, even this claim is not completely true, nor is it completely false. At any particular point in time it is merely true to *some degree*. And the closer the baby gets to the time of its birth, the more it becomes its own *separate* entity *apart* from the woman's body.

The abortion issue can be resolved by taking all of the relevant factors into account. When all the different degrees of "this and that" become established, legimetricians will be able to construct a set of "abortion curves." These curves will indicate the level of "murder" for aborting a fetus at any particular point in the pregnancy. It is important to remember that these curves will *not* define any kind of "boundary line" between what *should* be considered "murder" and what *shouldn't*. And so a person involved in an abortion will *not* be simply either "guilty" or "not guilty" of murder, but a mixture of *both*. They will be only *partially* guilty.

As an example, I have made an attempt at deriving a first-order approximation to the Realistic "abortion curve." (See Appendix.) The resulting curve is represented by the following table:

| Weeks since conception | Degree of murder | Penalty (days in prison) |
|---|---|---|
| 0 | 0.0 percent | 0 |
| 5 | 0.8 percent | 31 |
| 10 | 3.0 percent | 111 |
| 15 | 6.3 percent | 229 |
| 20 | 10.2 percent | 371 |
| 25 | 14.5 percent | 530 |
| 30 | 19.1 percent | 700 |
| 35 | 23.9 percent | 873 |
| 40 | 28.7 percent | 1048 |
| 45 | 33.5 percent | 1221 |
| 50 | 38.1 percent | 1389 |
| 60 | 46.7 percent | 1706 |
| 70 | 54.6 percent | 1992 |
| 80 | 61.5 percent | 2245 |
| 90 | 67.6 percent | 2465 |
| 100 | 72.7 percent | 2654 |

The left-most column indicates the number of weeks that have elapsed since conception. The middle column indicates the degree to which a murder has been committed if an abortion occurs at that time. The right-most column indicates the recommended prison term for the abortion (based on an arbitrary ten year prison sentence for a person who is 100 percent guilty of killing another human being). For brevity I have indicated only about 15 values in the table. Intermediate points can be found either by interpolation, or by evaluating the equation given in the Appendix.

188     *Shades of Reality*

The guilts and corresponding penalties expressed in the above table are *total* values for an abortion at the specified time. So these values are to be divided among the individual participants. For example if an abortion is performed after 25 weeks of pregnancy, the 530 day total prison term for that abortion would probably be split (in accordance with the Conservation of Crime and Guilt, as discussed in Chapter Ten) into a 265 day sentence for the woman, and a 265 day sentence for the doctor who performed the abortion.

The above abortion curve *does* take into account the pro-abortionist claim that a fetus is a part of a woman's body. Consequently, the degrees of guilt and corresponding penalties are initially somewhat lower than they would have otherwise been. However, the amount of this lowering diminishes as time passes (since the validity of the claim also diminishes with time).

Also notice that the degree of guilt does *not* reach 100 percent at birth (40 weeks). Instead the baby is still considered to be an incomplete human being even after it is born. For the next several years it will continue to develop into a more complete human being while it is *outside* of the womb. Consequently, the abortion curve extends past the normal 40 week gestation period in order to handle the possibility of *postnatal* "abortions."

Once again, the above table is only one suggestion for the abortion curve. You might want to try proposing your own curve. For example if you are having difficulty accepting the notion that a newborn baby is still not yet a complete human being, then you might prefer an abortion curve for which the degree of murder gradually reaches 100 percent by the time of *birth*. Or if you feel that the penalty for killing a *complete* human being should be more (or less) than ten years in prison, then you might want to adjust the values in the right-most column up (or down) appropriately.

Or if you are a "pro-choicer" who is still having difficulty dealing with the *realities* of abortion, you might feel more comfortable proposing a quasi-realistic abortion curve instead (simi-

*Abortion*     189

lar to the quasi-realistic voting curve that we saw in Figure 9.4 when we discussed the issue of minimum voting age, or similar to the quasi-realistic speeding curve shown in Figure 9.5). Then you could allow for a kind of "grace period" for abortions (perhaps several weeks from the time of conception), during which time there would be no penalties assessed. After the grace period expired, the prison term assessed for performing an abortion would gradually ramp up from zero. This solution would also satisfy the Prime Directive of Equality. But you would still be faced with the problem of establishing (and justifying!) the exact duration of such a grace period.

## Conclusion

I suspect that there will still be many readers who, because of their lifelong indoctrination to the Aristotelian way of thinking, will look at the Realistic abortion curve (or *any* abortion curve) and come to the "bottom line" conclusion that abortion must therefore be illegal. Otherwise, why would there be *any* prison sentences involved?

Let me reiterate. Abortion is neither legal nor illegal, but a mixture of both. If it *were* totally illegal, the prison terms for abortion would be much *longer*. The fact that they are as *short* as they are is an indication of the *legality* of abortion.

The pro-reality view regarding abortion does not coincide with either of the two currently popular views on the matter. (In fact, because the penalties are so lenient, the pro-lifers seem to regard pro-reality as siding with the pro-choice camp, while the pro-choicers feel just the opposite!) But correctness is not determined by *popularity*, but by *consistency* (see Chapter Zero). Therefore, the pro-reality view is the *correct* view because it is the only view that is consistent with reality. (The other two views aren't consistent with much of *anything*, except perhaps wishful thinking.)

## 190    *Shades of Reality*

Reality does not draw bivalent boundary lines between "day" and "night," or between "human being" and "non-human being." So rather than foolishly and ignorantly continuing to debate the exact moment at which "the sky becomes dark," let's begin to "see the light" instead. And having analyzed the matter in the light of fuzzy logic, we can now lay the abortion question to rest and (aside from a few quantitative aspects) regard it as being pretty much a dead issue (no pun intended).

# Chapter Twelve

# Rights and Equality

I have intentionally saved this chapter for near-last because it contains some of the most difficult and controversial concepts that result from applying the fuzzy paradigm to issues in American society.

Let us now consider that famous line that Thomas Jefferson wrote in the Declaration of Independence:

*We hold these truths to be self-evident, that all men are created equal, that they are endowed by their Creator with certain unalienable Rights, that among these are Life, Liberty, and the pursuit of Happiness.*

Of course, we know that everybody is *not* equal in terms of their physical attributes or intelligence or skills. We all have our individual strengths and weaknesses. (If everyone *were* exactly alike, then there would be no need, for example, to *elect* our government officials; we could simply choose them at random.) Instead, what Jefferson meant by "Equality" was that everyone is seen as being equal in the eyes of the law.

192    *Shades of Reality*

However, what may have seemed "self-evident" to Mr. Jefferson and his contemporaries is somewhat dubious in the light of the fuzzy paradigm. Since law is fuzzy (at least any kind of realistically meaningful law), then might not Rights and Equality also be fuzzy? Is every human being *exactly* equal, or is everybody just *almost* equal (i.e., equal "for all practical purposes")? The answer to the question depends on the interpretation of the word "human."

I strongly suspect that there are many readers (especially the anti-abortionists) who are still having trouble understanding the concept of "degree of being a human." They probably still think that something either *is* a human, or else it *isn't*. And even if it's only the *slightest* bit human, then it must be *100* percent human. (They are still *"drawing the line at zero,"* and then equifying.)

**Missing Links**

Unless you are a creationist, you probably accept the concept that all animals (including Man) are biologically related, and that all present-day animals evolved from older and more primitive forms of life. And even if the particular species *Homo sapiens didn't* evolve, there is still evidence that prehistoric humanoid creatures (such as Homo Erectus, Neanderthal, etc.) *did* once live on earth, regardless of *how* they got here.

In any event I would like to raise the question: If these creatures were still alive today, would they be considered to be "human beings," or would they just be another name on the endangered species list? Would killing one of them be considered "murder," or would it be considered as being nothing more than illegal "hunting"? Would they be granted equality with the rest of mankind? Would an eighteen-year-old member of their species have the right to vote if it lived in the United States? Would *any* of them even have *any* rights? Would we regard them as being our *peers,* or our *pets*?

*Rights and Equality*     193

Of course such creatures *don't* exist today, and so we can pragmatically avoid having to answer these questions. But consider the possibilities offered by the new field of genetic engineering. By slightly altering the structure of DNA it is possible, even today, to change the genetic characteristics of plants and animals. Someday it might even be possible to start with a *monkey* and end up with a *human being* by genetically creating the entire continuum of "missing links"! If this were ever accomplished, which of these new "species" would be *human* and which ones *wouldn't*? (An anti-abortionist, with his sorites-type of reasoning, would have to conclude that they would *all* be human, *including the monkey!*)

### "Human" Rights

If "rights" and "equality" are to be considered as all-or-nothing ideas, then where on the continuum of missing links would be the cutoff point separating those creatures that *have* rights from those that *don't*? Which creatures would have been created "equal" to Man, and which ones would have been created "unequal"?

We don't need to wait for the prospects of genetic engineering to come to fruition before we can start thinking about these kinds of questions regarding "human" rights. Even today we can ask: Is every person on earth totally "human"? How about a cold-blooded murderer, or a molester of children who feels no remorse for his actions? Are they to be regarded as being 100 percent human and given all the "Rights of Life, Liberty and the pursuit of Happiness," just because their bodies have an *anatomical* structure that we associate with the term "human being"? Or is there something more to being a human being than merely having a prescribed set of body parts?

On the other side of the coin, consider an anencephalic "person," one who is born *without* a complete brain and who

194　　*Shades of Reality*

therefore achieves little or no degree of consciousness. They too *look* human, at least on the outside. But then so does a Barbie doll. Can a living entity be considered to be human if it doesn't even have a human brain? Should such an entity be granted rights and be considered equal to someone *with* a brain? Should we even "feel sorry" for such an entity for its having to exist in such an unfortunate state? Should we feel sorry for a Barbie doll that loses one of its plastic arms?

Of course the first response that comes to mind is that a Barbie doll isn't something that's alive, and so the comparison is false. So let's ask the same kinds of philosophical questions about something which *is* living: Should we feel sorry for every *human egg* that goes *unfertilized*? After all, it too was deprived of the "Right" to develop into a complete human being.

And how about the other half of the component, the millions of potentially could-have-been human beings represented by un-used sperm? Shouldn't we also feel sorry for them? Shouldn't we feel obliged to bury each of these half-potentially human entities three feet underground in cemeteries (*semi*-teries?) and bring them half-bouquets of flowers while we kneel (on one knee) and cry tears from one of our eyes? Or should we, in our so characteristically Aristotelian fashion, simply "draw the line at zero" and have compassion for only those living entities that were lucky enough to become completely conceived?

**The Right To Life**

Consider the following somewhat far-fetched and admittedly contrived scenario: You have just built a time-travel machine, and you have gone back in time to the year 1932. As you wander around, you suddenly come upon a building which is on fire. On the roof of the burning building are two men trapped by the flames. One of the men is Albert Einstein. The other man is

*Rights and Equality* 195

Adolph Hitler. There is just enough time to rescue one, and only one, of the two men. Which man would you choose to save?

If you are a true believer in the notion of Aristotelian equality and the right to life, then you would have to flip a coin to decide. (Remember that in 1932 Hitler was not yet at war with the United States, and was therefore not an enemy.) But if you are honest and realistic in your assessment of the problem, you will easily realize that all human life is *not* equally valuable.

If the above scenario seems too unrealistic or too extreme, then consider the same scenario, only let it take place *today* instead of in 1932. Instead of Hitler and Einstein, let it be a schoolteacher and a drug pusher who are trapped.

Our society presently divides (and equifies) everyone into two distinct groups: Those who *have* the right to live (such as you and I), and those who *don't* (such as prisoners on death row). There is no middle ground. There are no shades of gray to that right. It is black and white. Everyone who has a right to life has exactly as much of that right as everyone else, be they saint or sinner, scholar or idiot, dope addict or drug pusher. And society seems to feel that all of these lives must be preserved *at all possible cost.*

Let's return for a moment to our discussion of the genetic engineering experiment and ask the question: Which of the "missing links" would have the right to life, and which ones wouldn't? Perhaps, in an attempt to avoid being forced into selecting an arbitrary cutoff point, you might now decide to "draw the line at zero" and adopt the strategy of claiming that *all living things* (not just all "men") are endowed by their Creator with the right to life. But that strategy (as we saw in the discussion of "pro-life" in the previous chapter) leaves *us* with very little to eat.

### The Right to Liberty

When a person commits a crime and is sent to prison for a brief term, he is partially deprived of his Right to Liberty. (I say

196    *Shades of Reality*

"partially" because the deprivation is not permanent — he will be released after his term in prison is over.) And even a convict out on parole is still not totally free. He must maintain contact with his parole officer, and he must refrain from participating in certain activities that would otherwise have been allowed had he not been on parole. So even under our present system of democracy the Right to Liberty is already clearly a matter of degree.

Even an honest "law-abiding" person who has never been arrested is not *totally* free. Most of us have to work for a living, perhaps doing jobs that we don't always enjoy having to do. Plus, we have obligations that we must honor to family, friends, and acquaintances.

Nor does the Right to Liberty mean that we can just come and go absolutely whenever or wherever we please. There are many "restricted areas" where only "authorized personnel" are allowed to enter.

### The Right to the Pursuit of Happiness

Of the three Rights mentioned in the quote from the Declaration of Independence, the Right to the pursuit of Happiness is probably the one that is most obviously fuzzy. As long as your Happiness occurs in complete isolation (or maybe in the presence of a consenting group), then the Right is fairly crisp. For example if you are at home and you want to watch a particular TV show, or read a certain book, or have sex with your partner, then you should have a high degree of Right to do so.

But quite often, *your* Right to the pursuit of *your* Happiness can conflict with *somebody else's* Right to the pursuit of *their* Happiness. For example it may give you Happiness to smoke cigarettes. Do you therefore have the Right to smoke? It just so happens that it gives *me* Happiness *not* having to breathe somebody's secondhand smoke (especially inside transportation vehicles and other areas of forced confinement). Do I not therefore

*Rights and Equality*     197

have the right to enjoy clean smokeless air? You want to smoke. I want you to *not* smoke. Once again we have the Aristotelian conflict between **A** and **not-A**. Therefore the Right to smoke is clearly a *fuzzy* Right.

But sometimes the fuzziness in the Right to pursue Happiness is not quite so immediately obvious. Should you have the right to use heavy drugs? The superficial answer might be that it should be entirely OK, since you would be only harming yourself and nobody else. (And it should never be illegal for anyone to harm *him/herself*.) But more often than not, the use of such drugs leads the user into a life of crime in order to get money to continue financing their addiction. Once again we arrive at a conflict between your Right to pursue drugs, and *society's* Right to not have to be *bothered* by you.

Since it should not be against the law for anyone to do potential harm to themself, there should not be laws requiring the use of seat belts or motorcycle helmets. If someone prefers to "pursue his happiness" in a foolish or risky manner, then that should be *his* business, as long as his actions don't endanger anyone else. It should not be the prerogative of the government to enact particular laws just because those laws might be "good for us." Otherwise, they might just as well start passing laws making it illegal to do such things as to eat candy or watch TV for prolonged periods of time, since neither of those activities is very good for us either.

### Fuzzy Rights and Fuzzy Equality

We have already pointed out that, even in the eyes of our present legal system, everybody most definitely does *not* have the same Rights and Equality. You remember that eighteen-year-olds have the Right to vote, but seventeen-year-olds *don't* have that Right. Therefore "we can hold this truth to be self-evident" that seventeen-year-olds are *not* created equal to eighteen-year-

## 198    *Shades of Reality*

olds! (Or, as George Orwell might have said, we may all be equal, but clearly some of us are *more* equal than others.)

Furthermore, it would seem that society already subconsciously acknowledges the idea of partial Rights. Hardly a day goes by without someone uttering an expression like, "You don't have *any* Right to do (such and such)." Notice the choice of the wording, "*any*" as opposed to simply saying "You don't have *the* Right." The word "*any*" automatically implies an acknowledgment of potential quantification.

As un-American as I know it sounds, we are eventually going to have to acknowledge the reality that every warm body on our planet is not *exactly* equal to every other warm body, despite Mr. Jefferson's claims to the contrary. The only way we're going to be able to provide meaningful and realistic answers to questions about rights and equality is to acknowledge those concepts in terms of shades of gray:

> ***If "human-ness" exists in degrees, then so too must human Rights and Equality exist in degrees.***

Furthermore, Rights and Equality are not concepts endowed on us by our *Creator*. They are concepts endowed on us by *ourselves*. And as such, we can adopt whatever rules we want for playing those kinds of games. But if we insist on trying to continue the games in an Aristotelian fashion, we are someday going to find ourselves facing the very same kinds of tough questions that the abortion issue used to face. If we proceed with genetic engineering and apply all of its potential, where will we "draw the line" between those life-forms that we will consider as being "human" (and which are therefore "equal" and "endowed with unalienable Rights"), and those that *just miss* falling into that prestigious category? And even if we never *actually perform* such experiments, we have still already opened up a Pandora's box merely by recognizing the *possibility*.

*Rights and Equality* 199

## Natural Rights and Natural Equality

Let's ask ourselves, how does nature (or physical reality) deal with the concepts of Rights and Equality? The answer is — it doesn't. Nature does not simply *endow* Rights to animals. All "Rights" have to be *earned*. If an animal wants the Right to life, then it must be clever and resourceful enough to keep itself from being eaten. Therefore, a sick or injured animal doesn't have exactly the same "Right" to life as a healthy one. Nature does not demand that a lion give fair and equal treatment to all animals, injured or not. An injured animal becomes the lion's dinner. In nature, the law is, "survival of the fittest."

That is also the principle behind the concept of natural selection in evolution. Those genetic traits that are beneficial to the survival of a species endure, and those that are not get eliminated. But by declaring everyone to be equal (and simply handing over "Rights" to everybody), mankind has stopped the natural selection process for the species *Homo sapiens*. Everyone is now *equally* "fit." Everyone survives to contribute to the gene pool. Evolution has been halted.

Or perhaps it would be more correct to say that evolution is now proceeding in a *haphazard* fashion now that natural selection no longer guides its direction. Instead of the undesirable traits being eliminated from the system, they are allowed to continue evolving along with the good.

In every biological system, be it a single cell, a complete animal, or an entire society, there is a need to eliminate waste material. Without a mechanism for removing such poisons, the system will eventually die. (In our bodies, our kidneys are a part of this waste-removal mechanism.) Natural selection may therefore be viewed as the "*kidneys of evolution.*" But now that its "kidneys" have been removed, how can we keep human evolution from becoming poisoned?

200  *Shades of Reality*

The first step is to recognize and accept the fact that some parts of the system *are* indeed simply waste materials that need to be eliminated. And since *we* are the ones responsible for the kidney-removal operation, it is now incumbent upon *us* to prescribe an appropriate method of dialysis. In other words, the future course of human evolution is now in our own hands.

In the past, the course of evolution was controlled entirely by nature (i.e., "natural" selection). While it was left to fate (or God) to decide who specifically would survive and who specifically would die, natural selection would help skew the statistics slightly in favor of those creatures having advantageous attributes. But now *we* have assumed a large portion of the role formerly played by God. Now when nature says to a person, "It's time to die," we step in with a wonder drug or a surgical operation and say "No." We keep the person living. But if we choose to step in and "play God" like that, then we must be prepared to play God at *both* ends. We must also accept the responsibility for willfully *terminating* lives as well as *saving* them.

**The Value of Life**

How much does a parakeet cost? Probably around ten or twenty dollars. How much does a puppy dog cost? Depending on what kind you buy, it might cost anywhere from a few dollars to a few hundred dollars.

But what's the value of a *human* life (in dollars)?

How many of you answered: "Priceless"?

How many of you said: "It depends on *whose* life it is"?

The species *Homo sapiens* likes to see itself as being infinitely valuable. In our minds, nothing in the whole universe is more important than *we* are. In fact, no other life form can even come close in comparison. There's simply no way to put a price tag on something as wonderful and perfect as *we*! (Do we have an ego problem or what!)

*Rights and Equality*     201

Let's see how much money our present *legal system* thinks a person's life is worth. Looking at the table of crimes that we saw back in Chapter Ten, we see that the penalty for killing someone (shown in the first three lines of the table) ranges anywhere from 3 years to life imprisonment, depending on the degree of murder. Recalling that each year in prison is approximately equivalent to the theft of about $1,000, your "infinitely valuable" life doesn't appear to be worth much more than a few thousand bucks!

## Controlled Evolution

Now that we can begin to see things in their proper perspective, let's return to our discussion about the elimination of waste material from our evolutionary development.

Of course we can't go around just killing each other "willie-nillie" (although the proliferation of hand guns and the increased number of drive-by shootings might suggest otherwise!) But we *can* decide what level of effort we wish to make at keeping alive the undesirable elements of our society. We *can* acknowledge that the Right to life in society (just as in nature) must be *earned* and not simply *granted*. And we *can* acknowledge the sobering reality that human life is *not* infinitely valuable, nor is it all *equally* valuable.

## Criminals

Let's start with our criminal justice system. Our society spends far too much time and money taking care of criminals. We give them food and shelter and see to it that they are reasonably comfortable. And after we've housed and fed them for a while we slap their hands and then send them back out to reinfect the community.

*And to what purpose?* Is it because we feel that society

## 202 *Shades of Reality*

*needs* to have troublemakers running around loose? Is their continuing existence on this planet accomplishing something so beneficial to society (and to the long-term evolution of mankind) that it must be endured in spite of the problems they create? In fact, wouldn't we all be much better off if we didn't have to waste time and money keeping these kinds of nuisances alive? (Try answers of "no, no, and yes," respectively.)

Everybody makes mistakes once in a while. But if the nature of a particular person is such that he chronically gets into serious trouble, or if he's foolish enough to allow himself to start taking drugs, then society should have very little interest in allowing him to contribute to the gene pool.

If we're going to take human evolution into our own hands, and if we're going to control the destiny of society, then let's start by eliminating the useless and smelly waste at the very bottom.

It just so happens that there is a very straightforeward way of accomplishing all of this without even violating the Prime Directive of Equality. It involves the concept of "fading out" (see Chapter Ten) coupled together with an increasing level of hardship. As the number of crime units for a criminal continues to increase, not only would the *duration* of each successive prison term increase, but its *severity* as well. For example we might simply start feeding them less and less with each new conviction until they actually *do* "fade away"! Or we might devise even more severe ways to make their prison stays increasingly miserable.

What's that? — "Cruelty," you say?

"Inhumane treatment," you mumble?

You're damn right!

It's about time we stop treating the scum of society as if they were honored house guests. They're supposed to be in prison, not on vacation with free room and board. But to appease the "bleeding hearts" of society, we *could* offer each prisoner the

*Rights and Equality* 203

ongoing option to request a more humane execution at any time. That way it would always be his choice whether he wants to continue suffering or not.

## Welfare

Since the Right to life should be earned and not simply bestowed, the welfare system should be little more than the equivalent of a federally operated insurance company. The purpose of welfare should be to provide *temporary* financial aid to the productive members of society who have earned the right to such assistance. It should *not* be a source of free funds for the derelicts of the world. The idea of "living on welfare" (except as a reward for past accomplishments) should be an absurdity. If a person cannot make it on his own, or if he cannot justify a valid reason for his continued existence, then he should be entitled to very little of the Right to life. (The world does *not* owe anybody a living.)

Of course it's not a requirement that a person *must die*, just because he fails to meet the prescribed qualifications for the Right to life. If the person's life is significant enough to someone *else* (such as a relative or a friend) who is willing to take the responsibility of supporting him/her, then that is an entirely different matter. His existence then *does* have a purpose — it provides happiness to his sponsor who, as a productive member of society, *does* have the Right to the pursuit of such happiness. But the burden of support is then *private* rather than *public*.

This option of allowing a person to have a sponsor clearly illustrates that all human life is *not* equal in value. It shows that:

> **The value of a person's life (as is the case with any commodity) is determined solely by how much somebody else is willing to pay for it.**

204    *Shades of Reality*

**Medical Care**

Just as with welfare, medical care should also be generally regarded as being a commodity of only short-term application whose primary purpose is to lead to an eventual healing of the patient. If a person is incapacitated and suffering from a terminal illness, then simply keeping that "warm body" alive is a waste of medical resources. There is a limit to how far we can be expected to go in our adopted role of "playing God." And even if we *could* keep a person alive forever, what would be the purpose? (If we had not stepped into our God-playing role, *nature* (or God Himself) would have probably killed off the person by applying the "survival of the fittest" rule. Then *we* would not have had to be responsible for the death.)

**Utopia**

By preserving only those attributes of humanity and those aspects of society that we perceive as being beneficial and desirable, we would once again be providing direction for the evolution of mankind and society. But instead of *natural* selection being the driving force behind evolution, as it was in the past, it would now be *human* selection.

In addition to the *long-term* benefits that would occur, the quality of life in society would *immediately* improve. Major crime would disappear virtually overnight. Crime cannot easily survive in a society that has no criminals. And (one way or the other!) criminals would surely cease to exist.

Without crime, the size of our police force could be cut dramatically. And police work would not be nearly as hazardous as it currently is. In fact, the role of a typical policeman would become little more than that of being a meter maid.

And finally, with poverty and the need for welfare eliminated, our country would enjoy a higher standard of living. By no

*Rights and Equality* 205

longer having to invest time, effort, and resources managing and maintaining the dregs of society, taxes could be greatly reduced. Instead of wasting revenues on taking care of criminals and perpetuating poverty by giving away welfare checks, tax money could be directed toward more productive efforts.

## Chapter Thirteen

# The End

In this final chapter we will try to investigate what the fuzzy paradigm can tell us about the final chapter of our *life* — namely, death and the hereafter — and what fuzziness reveals about religious concepts like souls, heaven, and hell.

### Death

Just as human life exists in degrees, so too does death. In fact it is just as proper to view the point of conception not only as the start of a person's *life*, but also as the beginning of that person's eventual *death*.

In the human body cells are constantly dying and new cells are continually being created to take their places. We are perpetually dying and being reborn, one cell at a time. And even when it appears that the *entire* body has died (no heartbeat and no respiration), oftentimes the person can still be revived by applying emergency techniques. (Usually after such revivals the victim reports having experienced the common hallucination of seeing a

*The End*　　207

bright light at the end of a tunnel accompanied by feelings of peace and serenity.)

Even the human brain does not die all-or-nothing. Kill a brain cell and the brain is still alive and functioning. (In fact brain cells die *naturally* all the time.) Kill another brain cell, and another, and another . . . . By the time you finish killing the last cell, the brain will have died. But there will be no one cell's death that would be responsible for the complete death of the entire brain. The brain would slowly change from a state of consciousness into a state of unconsciousness. And then what? What happens *after* you die? I'll return to this question shortly.

Since the start of a person's life can also be viewed as the start of their death, should the killing of any adult be considered equally bad as the killing of any other adult? For example, should the level of crime for killing a healthy twenty-five-year-old be exactly the same as the level of crime for killing a seventy-five-year-old suffering from terminal cancer? Crimes of *theft* are not all equal. (The theft of $10 is a lower level of crime than is the theft of $20.) Shouldn't the "theft" of a person's life be regarded similarly? The closer a person is to death, the less should be the level of crime for murder. Of course there is generally no way of knowing *exactly* how long a person would have lived had they *not* been murdered. But we know what the *average* life span is. So as a rough approximation we might estimate the number of years of "deprived life" based on the victim's age, just as we currently use a person's age to *guess* at his/her actual "maturity level" when it comes to issues like voting rights or the purchasing of tobacco products, etc.

**Souls**

In olden times, before the principles of modern chemistry and thermodynamics were known, heat was thought to be a kind of invisible fluid, which flowed from hot regions into colder

## 208 *Shades of Reality*

ones. When a combustible substance such as wood was burned, the invisible substance "phlogiston" was released to produce what was seen as fire.

In olden times, human consciousness was thought to be an invisible entity, which flowed into a person's body at the time of birth and remained with the person until the time of death. This "soul" would then flow out of the person's body and go to its bivalent reward (either heaven or hell), depending on how the person had lived his life.

Today, the phlogiston theory of heat has long been abandoned to a more realistic explanation (the kinetic theory of molecular motion). But the "phlogiston of the brain" (or "soul") notion still lingers on. Many human chauvinists claim that the species *Homo sapiens* is the *only* life-form on earth (or even in the *universe*) that has one of these invisible entities. (Boy, aren't *we* the lucky ones!)

One of the difficulties in discussing concepts such as "souls," "God," "sins," etc., is that almost everyone has his own definitions for such things. However, there seems to be a fairly general agreement (or at least an *implication*) that the term "soul" refers to some kind of conscious entity that is associated with "you." It is this "you" that supposedly goes to heaven or hell when you die. (If your soul were *not* a conscious entity, then it would make little difference to you whether or not your soul went *anywhere*, since "you" would not be experiencing the "going.")

The exact nature of consciousness is still not completely understood, but one does not have to resort to metaphysical or supernatural explanations. For example, the brain has often been compared to a computer. While such an analogy is admittedly a gross oversimplification, it does provide us with at least a crude understanding of how we might view the concept of consciousness (or souls).

In many respects a computer almost seems to have the ability to think on its own. Even today many computer programs

*The End* 209

have "user-friendly" interfaces that almost give the users the impression that they are talking to another "live person" inside the machine. One of the primary goals of the area of research known as "artificial intelligence" is to create a machine that actually *does* emulate human thinking.

In the 1930s Alan Turing proposed what has become known as the "Turing test" for artificial intelligence. Imagine an experimental setup consisting of two separate rooms with closed doors. Inside room A is a computer, and inside room B is a person sitting at a computer terminal. Outside of the two rooms another person (who we'll call "the experimenter") sits in front of two computer terminals, one of which is connected to the computer in room A and the other of which is connected to the terminal in room B (but the experimenter doesn't know which room contains which). The experimenter is allowed to communicate with the "occupant" of each room only *via* its corresponding terminal. His goal is to try to determine which room has the computer and which room has the human being. If no experimenter can unambiguously make this determination, then the computer will have successfully passed the Turing test for artificial intelligence. (Many experiments have actually been done to illustrate the expertise of computers on this kind of higher level. In one such experiment a computer was programmed to compose music in the style of Bach. When the resulting music was performed along with "human-written" music, most of the listeners in the audience could not discern which compositions were created by the computer and which ones were created by the human.)

Let's imagine now a computer whose software has just passed the Turing test (or which at least has come reasonably close to passing). Could such a computer be said to have achieved some degree of *consciousness*? How could you ever "know" one way or the other? If you were to pull the plug on the computer, would you be "killing" an intelligent being? If so, where would the consciousness (i.e., the computer software)

210    *Shades of Reality*

"*go*" when the bits in the computer's memory "evaporated"? Would they go to some "bit heaven" in the cyber-hereafter? Would reloading the program from disk represent "cyber-reincarnation"?

While the analogy is not perfect, the concepts of "souls" and "software" are probably quite similar. We can imagine our consciousness as resulting from some elaborate conscious-awareness "program" that's running in our brains. As long as we are alive and awake, we *think* — and therefore we *are*. But when we die and the conscious-awareness software "evaporates" from our brains (just as bits "evaporate" from a computer's memory when power is turned off), we *no longer* think — and therefore we *no longer* are.

It has been estimated that the human brain has the capacity to store about $10^{18}$ bits of information. If each bit were to be represented by a grain of sand 1 millimeter in diameter, it would take a cubical sandbox about a half of a mile on each side to contain this much sand. Presumably, all of the information that makes you "*you*" is contained in the patterns of ones and zeros represented by these bits.

It has even been suggested by at least one author (Kosko) that it might someday be possible to "download" these bits that make up "you" and store them in computer chips, thereby giving you immortality in silicon! You would never have to sleep or eat (or have sex!) or die. Your consciousness, all of your memories, all of your mannerisms, all of "you" would just go on forever. If they were to hook up a speech synthesizer, a microphone, etc. to the chip they would be able to talk to "you," and the chip would respond exactly like you did when you were still alive. Of course an interesting question would then present itself — if they downloaded your bits into *two separate* computers, which one would be the real "*you*"?!

My own personal view on the matter is that *neither one*

*The End*     211

would actually be "you." To illustrate, it might someday be possible to print out the entire DNA structure of a strawberry. It would probably take reams and reams of paper, but all of the genetic information for creating a strawberry would exist on those pages. But merely having the *information* is quite a different matter from having an actual *strawberry*. (I would very much doubt that eating the sheets of paper would taste the same as eating a real strawberry, even though "all of the information is there" in both cases!) So too with your brain. "You" are more than simply stored *information*. When your brain "meat" dies, "you" die. (But the silicon version of "you" would sure make one hell of a Turing-test-passer!)

For the benefit of those readers who might still believe in souls, let's consider once again our discussion in Chapter Twelve of the genetic engineering experiment that might someday produce a continuum of "missing links" between a monkey and a human. If only human beings have souls, then at what location on that continuum of creatures would be the cutoff point for being human *enough* to have a soul? Or is it possible that souls (like the concept of "human"-ness) have *degrees* of existence? Might a cat or dog, for example, have a certain non-zero amount of soul? After all, they too are probably aware of their own existence. Otherwise they wouldn't experience fear and other instincts for self-defense and survival. Should we therefore stop eating cows, chickens, and fish just because they too might have souls? Or is it OK to eat creatures that have souls? If so, then is it OK for a human being to kill and eat another human being?

Suppose that extraterrestrial life exists somewhere in the universe, and that there exists a species that is more advanced than we are. Might they claim that only *they* are advanced enough to have souls, just as we have done? Might they therefore feel that killing and eating *us* is morally acceptable? Would they even *have* moral codes?

## Morality

Moral goodness and badness are not things that exist in the physical universe. They are not tangible things that we can measure and hold in our *hands*. Instead, good and evil are intangible concepts that we hold in our *heads*. It is *society* that defines what is right and wrong, not God. When society declared ecology to be "in fashion," it suddenly became wrong to hunt whales. Fifty years ago almost nobody had even *heard* of the word, "ecology." Fifty years ago it was *not* wrong to hunt whales.

Is murder wrong? Most of us would say "yes." But how do we *know* it's wrong? Maybe it just *seems* to be wrong, just like the earth at one time *seemed* to be the center of the universe. What experiment can we perform to test for the wrongness of murder, to show that it either *is* wrong or *isn't* wrong?

One of the problems with moral claims is that they are extremely fuzzy. What exactly do we mean by terms like "murder" or "wrong" or "lie" or "fair." Exactly *where* in the gray area between "murder" and "self-defense" does "wrong" turn into "right"? All acts are right to some degree and wrong to some degree. All things are both fair to some extent and also unfair.

Our perceptions of these matters (right vs. wrong, fair vs. unfair, etc.) depend to some extent on which side of the fence we're on. Often we may judge someone else's actions as being wrong — until we find *ourselves* doing those actions. And then we search to justify to ourselves our own rightness. We say, "Oh, but now it's *different*. In *my* case I'm only doing . . .but in *his* case he did. . . ." We may even lie to ourselves to accomplish the justification.

## The *Modus Operandi* of God

Let's pretend for the moment that such things as souls *do* exist. And let's imagine that when a person dies, his or her soul

*The End*     213

*does* go to either heaven or to hell. (You can even include some third possibility such as limbo or purgatory if you wish.) An obvious question then becomes, how good (or bad) does a person have to be in order to just *miss* going to hell (or heaven, or limbo)? Where in God's mind is the Aristotelian cutoff point between eternal salvation and eternal damnation?

Criminals usually have a *modus operandi* — a repeating pattern to the types of crimes they commit. When a crime is committed and there are no suspects, police will often try to find potential suspects by investigating certain peculiarities of the case. If the crime was a bank robbery and if entry into the bank was accomplished by exploding a stick of dynamite at the front door, then the police might check their dossiers to see which previously convicted criminals have a *modus operandi* of robbing banks by using sticks of dynamite.

As we pointed out in Chapter One, everything in nature happens smoothly. Day gradually becomes night. Winter slowly becomes spring. There are no well-defined boundary lines between caterpillar and butterfly, between tadpole and frog. Nature does not divide God's work into bivalent categories. Only *Man* does that. The *modus operandi* of God is therefore "shades of gray."

So then why are heaven and hell such bivalent all-or-nothing concepts? Why would God create a fuzzy universe filled with shades of gray, and then create a purely Aristotelian afterlife? Such a fabrication is totally inconsistent with His *modus operandi*. Or could it be that God *didn't* create these concepts? Could it be that *we* created these ideas about heaven and hell to conform to our *own* bivalent mentalities?

If there really is a hell, it must be a place of *degrees*. (No, I don't mean that it must be a *hot* place!) There could not be just one generic "hell" into which everyone who has been "bad" simply gets dumped. There are *degrees* of badness. For example, there is "telling-a-lie" level of badness, and there is "murder"

214    *Shades of Reality*

level of badness. And only somebody with the mentality of an Aristotelian would even suggest that both are *equally* bad.

Similarly, heaven would also have to have many different levels of *reward*. Otherwise, my only concern would be that I live my life just "good enough" to barely make it in. (Any "extra" goodness on my part would simply be a wasted effort!) There would have to be an entire continuum of possibilities between total heaven and total hell in order to avoid violating the Prime Directive of Equality (a concept which a truly just God would surely have to acknowledge).


## Oblivion

But as much as I'd *like* to believe in such places, I'm afraid that heaven and hell are merely the creations of overactive wishful thinking — a kind of "Santa-Claus-is-watching-you" carrot that we've created to dangle in front of potential evildoers to keep them in line. We tell ourselves that death is simply leaving *this* world and going someplace *else*. And so we invented heaven and hell as mythical lands to which our mythical souls can be sent. It's certainly an attractive fantasy and one which anyone could relate to.

But the reality of death is probably not so charming and fathomable. Even though I have not yet died (at least not at the time of this writing!), I strongly suspect that death is nothing more than a brief period of suffering, followed by total *oblivion*. And oblivion is not something anyone wants to look forward to, not so much because it's *bad* — but simply because it's *nothing*.

Oblivion is not a place that you *go* to. Oblivion is simply total *nonexistence*. It's the complete *lack* of "you." Oblivion is the "you" that didn't exist one hundred years before you were born. It's being one of your brothers or sisters when you never had any siblings.

If oblivion is everyone's ultimate fate, then the concern for

*The End*     215

human suffering on earth is a completely *meaningless* endeavor! Let me explain what I mean.

Imagine that there exists an unusual anesthetic, one which allows a patient to remain conscious during an operation and feel all of the pain. But when the operation is over, the patient has absolutely no memory of *any* of it. (I am told by members of the medical profession that an anesthetic of this nature actually exists!) After the operation, the patient feels exactly the same as if a *traditional* anesthetic had been used. The big question now becomes, "Did the patient really suffer the pain of the operation"?

On the one hand, the patient *does* experience the pain and suffering at the time the operation is being performed. And the perceived pain at that time is very real. But after the operation is over, there is an entirely different perceived reality. The suffering of the past no longer exists. It doesn't even exist as a *memory* of the past. In fact, it might just as well have taken place in a totally different universe, or perhaps in a fictional story in which somebody else did the suffering. (When Donald Duck accidentally hits his finger with a hammer, does real pain actually exist?)

If suffering occurred, but there is no perception of that suffering after the fact, then no harm has been done. There is no need for anyone to be any more concerned about such suffering than they would be about the mythical sufferings of any fictional character. And if oblivion is each person's destiny, then there will be no memory of any of their earthly suffering either. So concern for such suffering on *our* part is therefore just as meaningless as in the case of the anesthetized patient.

Of course, all of this is just speculation. Nobody really knows for sure exactly what lies on the other side of that great Curtain of Death. Maybe there *is* a heaven. Maybe there *is* eternal life. Or maybe we all just come back as *cows*. I don't know. But whatever the ultimate truth is, I won't know it until I die. And when that time comes, all I can do is hope that there will still be a "me" left to *do* the knowing.

# Appendix

# Derivation of the Realistic Abortion Curve

Let H($t$) represent the degree of validity of the claim that the fetus is a human being (at any time, $t$). Let B($t$) represent the degree of validity of the claim that the fetus is a part of the woman's body (at the same time, $t$). Then, since the fetus must belong partly to itself and the rest to its mother, we have:

$$H(t) + B(t) = 1$$

To allow for exponential decay with time, let B($t$) be expressed in the form:

$$B(t) = e^{-kt}$$

where,

$$k = \text{an appropriate decay constant}$$

Therefore:

$$H(t) = 1 - B(t) = 1 - e^{-kt}$$

*Derivation of the Realistic Abortion Curve*     217

Since B($t$) represents a degree of *validity*, then 1 - B($t$) must represent the degree of *invalidity* of the claim. Therefore the product of H($t$) [the degree of being a human] times (1 - B($t$)) [the degree of *not* being a part of the woman's body] must equal the degree of murder, M($t$):

$$M(t) = H(t) \cdot (1 - B(t)) = (1 - e^{-kt})(1 - e^{-kt})$$

$$M(t) = (1 - e^{-kt})^2$$

By selecting different values of $k$, different possible "abortion curves" can be constructed. One such curve is presented as a table at the end of Chapter Eleven. If $t$ is expressed in units of "years" then the value of $k$ is on the order of 1.